FROM WHAT TRIBE WERE YOU BIRTHED?

UNDERSTANDING THE SIGNIFICANCE OF AARON'S BREASTPLATE

FROM WHAT TRIBE WERE YOU BIRTHED?

UNDERSTANDING THE SIGNIFICANCE OF AARON'S BREASTPLATE

ANN GWEN MACK

Copyright © 2015 Ann Gwen Mack

All rights reserved. No part of this book may be reproduced, distributed or transmitted in any form by any means, graphics, electronics, or mechanical, including photocopy, recording, taping, or by any information storage or retrieval system, without permission in writing from the publisher, except in the case of reprints in the context of reviews, quotes, or references.

Scripture marked AMP are taken from the Holy Bible, *Amplified Version*®. Copyright ©1954, 1958, 1962, 1964, 1965, 1987 by Zondervan®. All rights reserved.

Scripture marked CJB are taken from the *Complete Jewish Bible*®. Copyright © 1998 by David H. Stern. All rights reserved.

Scriptures marked GW are taken from the Holy Bible, *God's Word to the Nations*. Copyright © 1995 by Baker Publishing Group. All rights reserved.

Scriptures marked MSG are taken from the THE MESSAGE. Copyright © 1993, 1994, 1995, 1996, 2000, 2001, 2002 by Eugene H. Peterson. All rights reserved.

Scriptures marked NIV are taken from the Holy Bible, *New International Version*®, NIV®. Copyright © 1973, 1978, 1984, 2011 by Biblica, Inc.™. All rights reserved.

Unless otherwise indicated, scripture quotations are from the Holy Bible, King James Version. All rights reserved.

Published by: Purposely Created Publishing Group™
Printed in the United States of America

ISBN-10: 1-942838-42-5
ISBN-13: 978-1-942838-41-8

Special discounts are available on bulk quantity purchases
by book clubs, associations and special interest groups.
For details email: sales@publishyourgift.com or call **(888) 949-6228**.

For information logon to:
www.PublishYourGift.com

DEDICATION

THIS BOOK IS DEDICATED TO

My HEAVENLY FATHER who is the head of my life! In HIS persistence to reveal HIS unconditional love for me, HE continues to confirm the purpose of my existence beyond what others would have me to believe about myself – outside of HIS will for my life. I am truly grateful for HIS patience and the calling HE has placed on my life. It is HE who validates me!

◆ ◆ ◆

For by him were all things created, that are in heaven, and that are in Earth, visible and invisible, whether [they be] thrones, or dominions, or principalities, or powers: all things were created by him, and for him: And he is before all things, and by him all things consist. - **Colossians 1:16 – 17 (KJV)**

TO THE MEMORY OF

My Earthly mother, Ruby Hinnant Mack, who went home to be with the Lord on August 17, 2014 and did her best while on this Earth to shelter me from the cruelty of the world! She was passionate about life, and she endured much suffering while continuing to be a forgiving person. She was a fighter who taught me to never give up!

◆ ◆ ◆

I will stand my watch and set myself on the rampart, and watch to see what He will say to me, and what I will answer when I am corrected. Then the Lord answered me and said: "Write the vision and make it plain on tablets, that he may run who reads it. For the vision is yet for an appointed time; but at the end it will speak, and it will not lie. Though it tarries, wait for it; because it will surely come, it will not tarry. "Behold the proud, His soul is not upright in him; But the just shall live by his faith. - **Habakkuk 2:1-4 (NKJV)**

TABLE OF CONTENTS

Dedication v

Introduction 1
   Reality and the Brain 5

CHAPTER 1 — 11
  a) Mistaken Identity 12
  b) History: Yours or Mine 15
  c) Biblical History 18
     1. Mazzaroth 25
     2. Constellations: Story in the Sky 28

CHAPTER 2 — 31
The Awakening: Spiritual Consciousness .. 32

CHAPTER 3 — 41
Hebrew-Jewish Calendar 42

CHAPTER 4 — 53
  a) From Genesis to Revelation 54
  b) Order of Birth: Jacob's Sons 58
     1. There is Power in a Name 61

TABLE OF CONTENTS

   2. Order of Responsibility and Authority:

      Personality, Character Trait, and Symbolism 65

   3. The Twelve Tribes of Israel 85

   4. Land of Distribution 93

CHAPTER 5   97

The Breastplate of Aaron 98

CHAPTER 6   105

Conclusion 106

   a) Who Am I? 112

   b) The Tribe of Gad 115

CHAPTER 7 (Bonus)   119

APPENDICES 125

ABOUT THE AUTHOR 173

FROM WHAT TRIBE WERE YOU BIRTHED?

UNDERSTANDING THE SIGNIFICANCE OF AARON'S BREASTPLATE

And Aaron shall bear the names of the children of Israel in the breastplate of judgment upon his heart, when he goeth in unto the holy [place], for a memorial before the LORD continually.

- Genesis 28:29

INTRODUCTION

Honestly, it is becoming increasingly more difficult to confirm much of anything these days. For instance, much of what we should be able to rely on lacks a tremendous amount of integrity. A photo can be digitally altered to present a false truth. In the same way, a forensic laboratory analysis and report can be manipulated to give the result of a false positive.

Furthermore, in an attempt to manipulate the economy, man may attempt to drive the cost of a good or service for reaching the greatest gain or revenue possible, despite its quality. This strategy is directed by and geared towards those who are in positions of power to receive and redirect the flow of wealth in their favor – whether right or wrong! And just like anything else, those in positions of power have placed a value on all resources to include the human race thus causing me to question everything - even my very own identity!

With that said, a hierarchy of what is important and who is acceptable has been used to determine a person's value for years. When cultures set out to conquer and exile other cultures, for example, it is done as an attempt to change or erase the history of those who have been conquered and taken captive. Considering the advancement of modern technology, especially the Internet, finding information is not a problem; however, attempting to locate the original material of a text or witnesses of the TRUTH in order to validate that information is a big problem indeed!

Many rare books are out of print, which makes them hard to find, and scholars who are very passionate about learning and recording the truth are of a rare and dying breed as well.

My people are destroyed for lack of knowledge: because thou hast rejected knowledge, I will also reject thee, that thou shalt be no priest to me: seeing thou hast forgotten the law of thy God, I will also forget thy children. - **Hosea 4:6 (KJV)**

ANN GWEN MACK

After much pondering, research, and prayer, it has taken me quite a while (several years) to follow through with my God-given assignment to identify the original gemstones on the Breastplate of Aaron (Aharon), also referred to as the Breastplate of Righteousness, Judgment, or Decision. These very special gemstones represent one of each of the Twelve Tribes of Israel. Nonetheless, our Heavenly Father, the creator of heavens and Earth to include all that lies within (mankind, plants, vegetation and animals) and outside (the entire universe), is all-knowing (omniscient), almighty (omnipotent) and wonderful. HE rewards those who diligently seek Him (**Hebrews 11:6**).

HE is, by far, the most loving, caring and faithful man I know, and I appreciate how He was and is the same today, yesterday, tomorrow and always. And based on who HE is, it is not His desire that we be ignorant to the truth! HE wants all of us to come into the full knowledge and understanding of not only who HE is, but who we are in HIM, and HIM in us (our purpose for being and existing).

FROM WHAT TRIBE WERE YOU BIRTHED?

In my opinion, the greatest TRUTH is this: God is love! HE has a standard, and HE is about divine order! God's order is very simple; it is mankind who complicates everything by making things more difficult than they really are, but God's love for us is unconditional.

HE loves us no matter what! So when we are ready to wake from our dark slumber to see and accept, through God's eyes (and not the world's), the **reality** of that which has been placed in front of us, HE is there to lead us and guide us along the way to all truth while reassuring us that "***we can do all things through CHRIST who strengthens us***" (**Philippians 4:13**) in order to fulfill our destiny.

They are darkened in their understanding and separated from the life of God because of the ignorance that is in them due to the hardening of their hearts - **Ephesians 4:18 (NIV)**

ANN GWEN MACK

REALITY AND THE BRAIN

Reality, the quality or state of being actual or true, can be defined according to what experiences most impact a person! Mainly, this refers to our culture and the people, places and things we encounter within our environment that influence our experiences. Every experience (good, bad, or indifferent) is absorbed and imprinted in our hearts. Those experiences may be a matter of life or death to the soul, and thus can either strengthen or weaken the spirit. The mind, if not fully equipped to handle these experiences (which are significantly unique to how we are individually impacted), can interfere with our spiritual growth!

These experiences are then transformed into baggage; and, if not properly addressed, that baggage can easily continue to grow or fester, possibly overflow or spill-over. Should we decide to share our experiences with others, they may or may not be inclined to agree with what we view as being truth, especially if they have not experienced the same occurrences or events in their life and are therefore unable to relate them to what we have encountered!

FROM WHAT TRIBE WERE YOU BIRTHED?

Sometimes, the deeper or greater the pain and hurt that those experiences generate, the more real those experiences become! These experiences can help to shape our character, to include how we think or process information. Always remember this: Information (good, bad, true, false, or indifferent) is equivalent to knowledge, and knowledge is power. Nonetheless, depending upon how that information is used, it can be proven to be invaluable!

Not only so, but we know that suffering produces perseverance; perseverance, character; and character, hope. And hope does not disappoint us, because God has poured out his love into our hearts by the Holy Spirit, whom he has given us. - **Romans 5:3-5 (NIV)**

The brain receives and processes information according to how the brain is wired (our understanding or perception). Therefore, it is possible for two or more people to have the same experiences and be influenced or impacted differently. The brain, which is a human computer, houses cells called neurons. These neurons receive electrical impulses that are beneficial in sending messages to and from other neurons within the body, and, as information is processed, it is then transmitted or downloaded to other cells, organs, or parts of the body. Another analogy for this process would be the process of communication. Receptors, or stimuli, take ahold of the information by storing it in the mind and heart of a person as memory to be recalled later. The brain controls how the body functions or responds to the information it has received.

These functions can be best described as voluntary movements that regulate our involuntary activities such as breathing or sleeping. The brain, which operates as the basis of our human consciousness, stores our memories and allows us to feel emotions that are controlled by our experiences and contribute to our personalities so we can develop our character. This, in essence, is what affects our reality. Therefore, that which is "real" to me may not necessarily be as real to you and vice versa. However, the fact that you do not realize my experiences does not negate their validity.

> Do not be conformed to this world (this age), [fashioned after and adapted to its external, superficial customs], but be

transformed (changed) by the [entire] renewal of your mind [by its new ideals and its new attitude], so that you may prove [for yourselves] what is the good and acceptable and perfect will of God, even the thing which is good and acceptable and perfect [in His sight for you]. - **Romans 12:2 (AMP)**

Unfortunately, many things are not what they seem, and you must be willing to challenge everything the world has taught you to believe, based on God's standards. The greatest of the enemy's attacks is what our mind imposes upon us. Renewing your mind is the art of unlearning so we can relearn God's truth! Peter said, "***HIS divine power has given us everything we need for life and godliness through our knowledge of HIM who called us by HIS own glory and goodness. Through these HE has given us HIS very great and precious promises, so that through them you may participate in the divine nature and escape the corruption in the world caused by evil desires***" **(II Peter 1:3-4)**.

As God reveals the topics that HE commissions me to expound on and to share with others, HE first ministers to me in confirmation of HIS plan for my life. Then, in turn, HE ministers through me to others. This is truly what I believe is meant by the saying "being blessed to be a blessing to others," especially when I have yet to realize my own potential and still question my ability to be used by God in amazement. Even as I hesitate to quickly put pen to paper in order to complete what HE has entrusted to me in a timely manner, as assigned, HE keeps on blessing me by encouraging me to open my heart and my mind to receive what HE has for me and to keep moving forward. HE never seems hesitant, put-off, or impatient with me.

To the contrary, HE relentlessly continues to communicate HIS expectation of what HE wants conveyed to me and through me in spite of what others would want me to believe. So HE pushes me forward IN LOVE while using scripture to communicate and reiterate HIS TRUTH and to drown out the noise in my head so I can realize (confirm) the importance of each God-given assignment, including my value!

> *"But ye are a chosen generation, a royal priesthood, a holy nation, a peculiar people;*

FROM WHAT TRIBE WERE YOU BIRTHED?

that ye should shew forth the praises of him who hath called you out of darkness into his marvellous light; which in time past were not a people, but are now the people of God: which had not obtained mercy, but now have obtained mercy." (1 Peter 2:9-10). *For "Ye have not chosen me, but I have chosen you, and ordained you, that ye should go and bring forth fruit, and that your fruit should remain: that whatsoever ye shall ask of the Father in my name, he may give it you."*
- **John 15:16**

CHAPTER 1

Don't fret or worry. Instead of worrying, pray. Let petitions and praises shape your worries into prayers, letting God know your concerns. Before you know it, a sense of God's wholeness, everything coming together for good, will come and settle you down. It's wonderful what happens when Christ displaces worry at the center of your life.

- Philippians 4:6-7 (MSG)

FROM WHAT TRIBE WERE YOU BIRTHED?

MISTAKEN IDENTITY

Cloaked in darkness for longer than I have embraced the light, years of negative mental conditioning outside of God's will often leads me to gravitate towards the familiarity of what binds me, rendering me ignorant of my purpose. But due to God's persistence, HE uses this season to reveal my true identity (self) to me. This is the reason for the birthing of this topic and the unfolding of our connection, through Biblical genealogy, to the Twelve Tribes of Israel! From the day we are birthed in the world, we cling to and rely on our Earthly parents to forge a connection with the family that God has pre-selected for us. In some cases, a bond is formed without conflict; however, in many cases, like perfect strangers we meet along our journeys called life, those we call family can be just as distant as strangers. The more I sought spiritual enlightenment, the more out of place and disconnected I felt from my natural, dysfunctional family habitat, thus leaving me alone and rejected.

Feeling like an outsider only made me more inquisitive about my Godly connection! As more truth was revealed to me, the more I had evolved in c h a n g i n g my way of thinking, also known as my mindset. With a newly developing mindset, my actions differed in how I responded to others, thus making me less recognizable or familiar to family and some friends. Let me explain! Over time, through a series of life events called tests (also known as trials and tribulations), we encounter experiences designed to wake us from our slumber. Some of us are actually revived or restored and move onward to fulfill God's will in reaching our destiny. However, some may find it more difficult to bounce back and move forward to see things differently, so they never change. Instead, they adapt to the world's system and never follow through with God's plan for their life.

Should we fail to read, study and learn for ourselves to know truth, we not only miss out on discovering the limitless hidden treasures within the Bible, but we also run the risk of being deceived by those who desire to keep us from learning who we should be! Why? Because not only is there power, purpose and meaning in a name, there is also power in knowing who you are (as God sees you)! And yet, for some reason, still searching for the resemblance or identity of my natural family bloodline and longing for that connection to the spiritual calling and gifting on my life, I directed my questions to God! I said, "God, where did my thirst and intensity for wanting to live my life according to your will emerge? Was it through my mother or my father? From which side of my family did this seed flourish?" And God gently told me that HE was going to take me back to the beginning, back to the Twelve Tribes of Israel, to show me where I fit! What an interesting and overwhelming perspective it is to see the root of your beginning, the history of your existence!

ANN GWEN MACK

HISTORY: Yours or Mine?

If you were to take a long and hard look at the word "history," you would see two entirely different words: **"his" and "story**." If you think about it, it makes sense! Is my story your story, or is your story my story? No, not exactly! My story hinges on my experiences, and your story, I am sure, is linked to your experiences. But for some reason, because many people find it hard to believe truth as it relates to me, they want to rewrite my story! In fact, they are often adamant, and sometimes indignant, on insisting that they can tell me that my story is a lie. And if I allow that manipulation and intimidation to form, I am denying my existence and myself. Why? Because for years I agonized over my reason for being, down to the exact year, month, day and time of my birth! I questioned my purpose as it related to the heart God gave me, a heart so easily broken and hurt by the level of unrighteousness in the world! And I could not seem to bring myself to do to others what was so easily done to me. I would often cry and ask God why HE had given me such a heart that prevented me from being like so many others in the world who gave no thought to their actions or their consequences. During the unfolding of my true identity, God revealed the answer and simply said I was not created to be like everyone else; I was fashioned with a "sensitive" heart for HIM and others!

If you were not present during my experiences, and in sync with my SPIRIT to feel the impact these experiences have had on me as they touched my heart, my mind and my soul like the experiences of my ancestors, then who are you to tell me that my story is a lie? Or is it that you were a negative part of my experiences, wanting people to see you, not as the person you were, but as the person you thought you had become? Yes, your past is your past; however, it is still a part of who you are, especially if you attempt to lock away secrets deep inside the darkness, where you think they are safely tucked away. ***There is nothing hidden that will not be disclosed, and nothing concealed that will not be known or brought out into the light (open) - Luke 8:17***.

Unfortunately, throughout time, people have attempted to rewrite history to deny the existence of God, heaven and hell. Often, as man begins to tamper with things to erase history by redirecting or restructuring his lies to resemble a false truth, he misses something! You *must* be willing to seek out the hidden treasures (or clues) in the midst of the darkness by starting at the beginning to learn who you were created to be!

You must forever keep in mind, as referenced in **Colossians 2:1-4, *God wants us to realize that HE continues to work as hard as HE knows how for us to include the Christians over at Laodicea.*** Not many of us have met HIM face-to-face, but that doesn't make any difference. Know that HE's on our side, right alongside us. We're not in this alone. He wants us woven into a tapestry of love, in touch with everything there is to know of HIM. Then we will have confident minds which are at rest, focused on Christ and God's great mystery. All the richest treasures of wisdom and knowledge are embedded in that mystery and nowhere else. And we've been shown the mystery! HE's telling us this because HE doesn't want anyone leading us astray and off on some wild-goose chase, after other so-called mysteries, or "the Secret."

FROM WHAT TRIBE WERE YOU BIRTHED?

BIBLICAL HISTORY

Christ spoke Aramaic, which is a combination of Greek and Hebrew, which was the language of the Jewish people in Biblical times. In accordance to Jewish history, during the start of the Babylonian exile, the use of Hebrew started to decline amongst Jews, and the Aramaic language became more widespread. Many Theologians have noted that during the pre-Reformation history of the Bible from 1,400 BC to 1,400 AD, the Old Testament was written in Hebrew and the New Testament in Greek. A Septuagint translated version came about somewhere between 300-200 BC. The Merriam-Webster dictionary references the Septuagint (from the Latin *septuaginta*, meaning "seventy," and frequently referred to by the roman numerals LXX) as being the earliest existing Greek translation of the Old Testament from the original Hebrew text.

The commissioning of the King James Version (KJV), commonly known as the Authorized Version (AV) or King James Bible (KJB) English translated version was believed to have begun in 1604 and was completed in 1611.

To date, the Bible has been translated in *over* 400 different languages and dialects. Unfortunately, the further removed something is from its origin, the greater the loss of its true meaning. In other words, when something is rewritten and translated from one language to another, it takes on an entirely different meaning. The confusing and recognizable so-called "errors, contradictions, and discrepancies" are the result of man's subsequent interference with the translation or transmission of the text, including man's failure to understand not only what is written, but also his attempt to impose his own views or understanding on others. This equates to many things being misconstrued and changed over the years from its original content and order, from one translation to the other. Regardless, the Bible, which is the word of God, is perfect in its original text! **Deuteronomy 4:2** states "***Do not add to what I command you and do not subtract from it, but keep the commands of the LORD your God that I give you***." Yet, many have done just that—subtracted and added to the word of God!

In spite of my frustration, my obedience to follow through with my assignment is very important! Moving forward, I shared my disappointment with God and consulted with the Holy Spirit for direction. Immediately, I was encouraged to review the names of both the Tribes of Israel and precious gemstones in the native Hebrew, Babylonian and Greek languages for a more accurate translation and comparison of the modern English names, spellings and meanings. First, God directed me to **Deuteronomy 8:7-9,** which describes Canaan as the land whose soil was enriched with iron, cooper and tin. Geographically speaking, the soil in different areas of the world may possess more or less various minerals while also yielding a variety of different types of gemstones per location. During this timeframe in ancient Egypt, silver was also highly regarded as having a greater value than gold, and trace amounts of copper, gold and silver were combined to form a widely used alloy called "electrum." Copper was the most important metal for making tools in ancient Egypt, and it was smelted in furnaces so that it could be extracted from malachite ore mined in the Sinai region. Malachite is a green copper carbonate hydroxide mineral with a chemical composition of $Cu_2CO_3(OH)_2$.

This precious gem was, unfortunately, very often mistaken for emerald. In its natural raw unpolished form, malachite is actually a softer stone. All specimens of this mineral are a striking lustrous green ranging from a pastel green, to a bright green, and to an extremely dark green that is almost black. It was also widely used for its healing properties, in addition to being used as an art medium for painting and eye makeup.

Knowing the chemical composition of the minerals, or the presence of certain elements, helps to determine or confirm the type of stones placed on the Breastplate, including the specific colors. For instance, the presence of copper in some stones contributes to its green tint, while tin can be combined with copper to produce a bronze or brass tint. The presence of iron in some gemstones contributes to the presence of a red tint or hue. Then God reminded me of the era in which these gemstones were collected or mined to construct the Breastplate. If each of the names of the Twelve Tribes was to be engraved on the gemstones, the hardness of the stones had to be soft enough for the names to be clearly seen. Many gems are classified by their translucency and hardness, which is determined in accordance to something called a Mohs scale.

Diamonds, composed of carbon, are known to have the greatest hardness at a measurement of 10, making them not easy to cut or engrave. Second to Feldspar, quartz is the most abundant mineral found in the Earth's continental crust. It is composed of silicon dioxide, the chemical formula of SiO_2. It consists of large traces of aluminum; sometimes it contains traces of potassium and calcium too. In some geographical areas, quartz may contain very small amounts of iron. What's known today as clear crystal quartz was called rock crystal, ice crystal and imitation diamond in ancient times. Another mineral more widely used by many cultures, including Ancient Egypt, Mesopotamia, Ancient Rome, and the Byzantine Empire, which resembled imitation diamond, rock crystal and moonstone was selenite, a fibrous, soft sulfate gypsum (also referred to as a form of alabaster). It is composed of calcium sulfate dehydrate and has the chemical formula $CaSO_4 \cdot 2H_2O$ with a hardness of 2 on the Mohs scale. Selenite ranges from a variety of colors—from being colorless or clear like water, to white, yellow, tan, blue, pink, brown, reddish,

reddish brown, or gray—due to the presence of impurities or the inclusion of other minerals. It is considered to be highly soluble and should it be worn in the rain as a piece of jewelry, it will dissolve or dissipate.

When your mind is open and you are receptive to hearing, listening and seeing the presence of the Lord in every aspect of your life, you will be amazed at what is revealed to you!

In fact, let's review 1 Corinthians 2:6-13 of the Message Bible which states, ***"We, of course, have plenty of wisdom to pass on to you once you get your feet on firm spiritual ground, but it's not popular wisdom, the fashionable wisdom of high-priced experts that will be out-of-date in a year or so. God's wisdom is something mysterious that goes deep into the interior of his purposes.***

You don't find it lying around on the surface. It's not the latest message, but more like the oldest—what God determined as the way to bring out his best in us, long before we ever arrived on the scene. The experts of our day haven't a clue about what this eternal plan is. If they had, they wouldn't have killed the

FROM WHAT TRIBE WERE YOU BIRTHED?

Master of the God-designed life on a cross. That's why we have this Scripture text:

No one's ever seen or heard anything like this,

Never so much as imagined anything quite like it—

What God has arranged for those who love him. But you've seen and heard it because God by his Spirit has brought it all out into the open before you.

The Spirit, not content to flit around on the surface, dives into the depths of God, and brings out what God planned all along. Whoever knows what you're thinking and planning except you yourself?

The same with God—except that he not only knows what he's thinking, but he lets us in on it. God offers a full report on the gifts of life and salvation that he is giving us. We don't have to rely on the world's guesses and opinions. We didn't learn this by reading books or going to school; we learned it from God, who taught us person-to-person through Jesus, and we're passing it on to you in the same firsthand, personal way."

Did you know that the Hebrew language was written and read from the right to the left, compared to left to right in the English language? When the original text was translated, that important fact was often forgotten, and much of the text's order was distorted or changed. This included the birth order of Jacob's children, the order of the gemstones on the Breastplate, and the encampment order of the Twelve Tribes. This not only contributed to my procrastination, but also my frustration and fear of not being able to execute what God commanded of me. Staying on course, I became more and more fascinated with the proposed correlation of the order of the birth of Jacob's sons with the sacred (Biblical) order of the months. Also, there is a distinct link or connection between the months, gemstones and zodiac signs as recognized by astrologists today.

♦ MAZZAROTH

Astrology is the study of the positions and relationships of the sun, moon, stars and planets, which have the ability to exert a strong influence over a person and contribute to their behavioral patterns. Frances Rolleston quite elegantly stated,

FROM WHAT TRIBE WERE YOU BIRTHED?

"Astrology is man's corruption of astronomy, as idolatry is man's corruption of religion; both originated from the truths they perverted and testify to the beauty." Unfortunately, there seems to be an increasingly deep-rooted connection to the darkness that drives man's prideful nature to arrogantly deny the perversion that he creates and claims as being *his* brilliant discovery. For example, there is a claim that positions of the heavenly bodies at an individual's birth may determine his or her basic personality or character traits. And sudden changes in astral positions or shifts during the course of a year cannot only be used to predict future events, but behavioral changes in individuals as well.

Nonetheless, the above concept of astrology as a means of determining who we are greatly contradicts **Jeremiah 1:5**, which states, *Before I formed you in the womb I knew [and] approved of you [as My chosen instrument], and before you were born I separated and set you apart, consecrating you; [and] I appointed you as a prophet to the nations (AMP)*. Thereby, God created us at a specific time for a purpose, and we are not defined solely by the position of the stars, the sun, and the moon in heaven on the day of our birth! All the signs of the stars, the moon, and the sun are in the hands of the Lord! The creation of the heavens and the stars as used in the practice of astrology was never intended for divination (**Deuteronomy 4:19, 2 Kings 23:5 and Isaiah 47:13**).

The stars were created by our Heavenly Father for declaring HIS glory and to aid us in keeping and tracking time in accordance to the seasons. *And God said, "Let there be lights in the expanse of the sky to separate the day from the night, and let them serve as signs to mark seasons and days and years, and let them be lights in the expanse of the sky to give light on the Earth." And it was so. God made two great lights--the greater light to govern the day and the lesser light to govern the night. He also made the stars. God set them in the expanse of the sky to give light on the Earth, to govern the day and the night, and to separate light from darkness. And God saw that it was good. And there was evening, and there was morning--the fourth day* (**Genesis 1:14-19**).

The Hebrew name for the zodiac is the Mazzaroth, meaning "constellations for story in the sky."

FROM WHAT TRIBE WERE YOU BIRTHED?

Canst thou bring forth Mazzaroth in his season? Or canst thou guide Arcturus with his sons? (**Job 38:32**)

The Bible, which contains Holy Scriptures, is full of history and prophecies to aid you in unraveling the hidden mysteries of a piece of a puzzle. Arranged in the perfect order, the zodiac tells the story of the birth, death and resurrection of our Lord and Master, Jesus Christ, the Redeemer! *And they [earnestly] remembered that God was their Rock, and the Most High God their Redeemer* (**Psalms 78:35, AMP**)

◆ **CONSTELLATIONS:** Story in the Sky
The Gospel of Jesus Christ and the Progression

The sufferings of Christ

1. **VIRGO**: Woman bearing the seed, the branch or vine; offspring. The seed of the woman shall come. [Birth]

2. **LIBRA**: Balancing the scales; the wages of sin; sacrificial offering. There shall be a price paid by Him for a purchased possession.

3. **SCORPIO**: Spiritual warfare; the ultimate battle of conflict. The price shall be a conflict with the serpent-foe and a wound in the conqueror's heel.

4. **SAGITTARIUS**: The archer; symbol of a warrior and conqueror. He shall be sent forth swiftly, surely, as an arrow from a bow. He who is sent!

The Redeemed

5. **CAPRICORN (US)**: The atoning sacrifice; wounded for our transgressions. He shall be slain as a sacrifice. Life comes from death; born to die with purpose!

6. **AQUARIUS**: Christ, the living water. The cleansing; born again (rebirth). He shall rise again and pour out blessings on His people.

7. **PISCES**: Uniting, the outpouring of the Holy Spirit and coming together. His people shall be multitudes held in union with each other and God.

8. **ARIES**: Overcoming and triumphant. He who was slain, whose heel was bruised, shall rule and shall tread His enemy under foot.

FROM WHAT TRIBE WERE YOU BIRTHED?

The Glory Redeemer

9. **TAURUS**: Inheritance. He shall come in power and have dominion.

10. **GEMINI**: He shall be the Son of God and the son of man, the victim and the ruler.

11. **CANCER**: Gaining momentum; victorious. He shall hold fast His purchased possession, the reward of His work.

12. **LEO**: He shall finally put all enemies under His feet, coming with ten thousand of His saints to execute judgment upon all, separating the evil from the good; resurrection.

CHAPTER 2

*Jesus answered,
Verily, verily, I say unto thee,
Except a man be born of water and of the Spirit,
he cannot enter into the kingdom of God.*

- JOHN 3:5 (JKV)

FROM WHAT TRIBE WERE YOU BIRTHED?

THE AWAKENING: Spiritual Consciousness

When a series of terrorist attacks took place, the year was 2001 and the date September 11th. I was employed by The Salvation Army at the National Headquarters in Alexandria, Virginia. The target of these attacks was the World Trade Center (WTC) in New York City (NYC), the Pentagon, and the United States Capitol in Washington, DC (DC). According to the media, American Airlines Flight #11, United Airlines Flight #175, American Airlines Flight #77, and United Airlines Flight #93 were hijacked by 19 al-Qaeda terrorists with the intent of sacrificing themselves in honor of their cause against the United States.

The objective of the initiated plan was based on their willingness to go down with the plane and take as many people with them while also forcing the pilots of each plane to fly into each building. With so much devastation in progress, people were frantically trying to reach their loved ones, who were physically present at the sites of the attacks. Many efforts were exercised in the hope of obtaining information that would lead to the whereabouts of family members and significant others in order to bring about peace and comfort to their mind, heart, and spirit!

This tragic incident brought many unlikely people together who assisted with the recovery efforts. Even the Salvation Army (TSA), to my understanding, was contacted by the White House via former President Bush to see if they would be willing to organize groups of people to help. So off I went!

> *And the LORD said unto Cain, Where [is] Abel thy brother? And he said, I know not: [Am] I my brother's keeper?* - **Genesis 4:9**

Initially, I was asked if I would be willing to assist those assigned to a temporary morgue. However, after learning that I would have to view cadavers and body parts while trying to create a list of items needed to aid people in claiming those impacted by the attack, I quickly asked if there was something else I could do. Having to view a finger or an arm and describe in detail the jewelry or noticeable tattoos was not something I thought I could forget without having nightmares about it for the rest of my life! I graciously accepted to be reassigned to the hospitality tent.

For approximately three to four weeks, I left my hotel room in New York City to take a ride on the train to the WTC to help in any way possible. Needless to say, my motives, in part, were due to my need for a temporary escape and change of scenery. Much later, it became clear to me that it was likely not my idea to volunteer as part of the WTC disaster recovery and cleanup efforts, but God's. God had an ultimate plan or reason for me being in the right place at the right time so I could receive a wonderful gift!

What a supernatural experience it was that jumpstarted a spiritually rewarding shift in my life! I have not been the same since my journey to NYC, not after being introduced to something called the "presence of energy through discernment."

> It's clear that we don't live to honor ourselves, and we don't die to honor ourselves. If we live, we honor the Lord, *and if we die, we honor the Lord. So whether we live or die, we belong to the Lord. For this reason Christ died and came back to life so that he would be the Lord*

of both the living and the dead. – **Romans 14:7-9**

It wasn't just any kind of energy! It wasn't physical or natural energy; it was supernatural energy that was detected by way of my gifting—high spiritual sensitivity. Put another way, it was the discernment of spirits or souls hovering all around me, the souls of those who had experienced a horrific death and refused to move onward! How can you prepare yourself for or fight against that which you cannot see? Although I was not able to see them with my naked eye, my spirit— the HOLY SPIRIT who dwells within me—put me on alert in being able to discern the unseen. Then God used me to pray for the dead, asking that they be allowed to follow the light and pass over to the other side so they could rest. Afterwards, HE arranged for me to meet Wanda Coleman, who was referred to as a spiritual counselor, to enlighten me about what I had encountered and why!

That day, she talked to me about the difference between religion, spiritualism, and metaphysics, explaining how they all overlapped and compared to one another. She also talked to me about the

Bible and how the supernatural was more real than the natural, saying that God gives us everything we could ever need or dream of in order to be victorious in spiritual warfare.

> *For I know the thoughts and plans that I have for you, says the Lord, thoughts and plans for welfare and peace and not for evil, to give you hope in your final outcome. Then you will call upon Me, and you will come and pray to Me, and I will hear and heed you. Then you will seek Me, inquire for, and require Me [as a vital necessity] and find Me when you search for Me with all your heart.* - **Jeremiah 29:11-13**

What I thought was a simple cleanup mission was God's way of getting my attention, waking me up and introducing me to something far greater: my purpose for being! So at the end of my shift at the World Trade Center each day, Wanda would retrieve me to educate me while taking me on a tour of the NYC area from one spiritual and metaphysical store to the other. Browsing one after the other, she educated me about the importance of scoping out the land and discerning spirits to what books to purchase to aid me in my spiritual quest. I became the model student, while listening and taking as many notes as possible. Returning to the Washington, DC, area, I became obsessed with seeking truth. My curiosity for learning more about God was heightened, and I wanted to see HIM and to experience HIM in every area of my life. I wanted to know how HE was connected to everything within and outside of the universe, and I was even more fascinated to learn about HIS connection to astrology, gemstones and numerology, which was birthed long before I was born and dates as far back to the creation of the world as particularly referenced during the period of Moses and his brother, Aaron. God's ways are not our ways, and our ways are not HIS, but everything created by HIM, man has been imitated and perverted in the name of religiosity and tradition! Can you imagine having an urge for certain knowledge and finally coming to understand its origin and connecting the dots, realizing that it is more than you ever imagined?

FROM WHAT TRIBE WERE YOU BIRTHED?

In whom also we have obtained an inheritance, being predestinated according to the purpose of him who worketh all things after the counsel of his own will: That we should be to the praise of his glory, who first trusted in Christ. - **Ephesians 1:11-12**

◆ ◆ ◆

My experience in New York City triggered in me an unquenchable thirst for seeking God in ways that my family did not understand. At every opportunity afforded to me, I needed to be in the house of the Lord, so I went out on a mission to devise a schedule for attending a service somewhere and anywhere seven days a week in search of my true identity in CHRIST. What knowledge I was not able to obtain from a Christian study group, I sorted from various books that God directed me to read. This led me on a quest to de-program what I thought I knew and replace it with what God needed me to know. This is when I truly learned and realized that man has a knack for perverting everything that God puts before us, changing the meaning and order of things to fit his own agenda.

As referenced above, did you know that, in modern times, the order of the months of the year as observed by man is not the original Biblical order that God intended us to recognize? March was the first month of the year, not January, based on a lunar-solar (moon-sun) system! Is it not obvious how we have been deceived? **Daniel 7:25** references and states how "*He* (**the adversary of the Most High God**) *will speak against the Most High God, oppress the holy people of the Most High, and plan to change the appointed times and laws. The holy people will be handed over to him for a time, times, and half of a time*.

Did you also know or realize that it is often impossible for a person to maintain a lie without the truth being revealed? That which is done in the dark will soon come to light (See Luke 8:17). And a half-truth is always a lie no matter how much the lie is twisted to resemble the truth! Therefore, telling part of the story is still a lie, which is why God tells us that HE would prefer we be "hot or cold; not lukewarm!" There is no in between or acceptable grey area!

FROM WHAT TRIBE WERE YOU BIRTHED?

A false witness shall not be unpunished, and [he that] speaketh lies shall perish. **Proverbs 19:9 (KJV)**

CHAPTER 3

And God said, Let there be lights in the firmament of the heaven to divide the day from the night; and let them be for signs, and for seasons, and for days, and years: And let them be for lights in the firmament of the heaven to give light upon the Earth: and it was so. And God made two great lights; the greater light to rule the day, and the lesser light to rule the night: he made the stars also. And God set them in the firmament of the heaven to give light upon the Earth, and to rule over the day and over the night, and to divide the light from the darkness: and God saw that it was good.

- **GENESIS 1:14-18 (KJV)**

FROM WHAT TRIBE WERE YOU BIRTHED?

HEBREW – JEWISH CALENDAR

The Jewish calendar, also known as the Hebrew calendar, is based on a lunar-solar system. For a better understanding, let's review the differences. A lunar calendar system is based on the movement of the moon around the Earth, which is observed each month at the start of a new moon when the first sight of moonlight or silver becomes visible after the dark of the moon. On the day of a new moon, the moon rises when the sun rises, and it sets when the sun sets. It crosses the sky with the sun during the day. The cycle takes a little less than 30 days (approximately 29½ to be exact) to complete. The Mayan civilization utilized a lunar calendar that they believed was related to the length of pregnancy and the length of time between planting crops and harvesting.

The modern civil calendar, also known as the Gregorian calendar, is widely recognized and used by most of the world today, but, unlike other calendars, the Gregorian calendar is based on a solar system of measurement. In using this type of calendar, we have abandoned any correlation between the moon cycles and the month, arbitrarily setting the length of months to be 28,

30 and 31 days. This calendar does take into consideration the seasonal changes, which are in harmony with the apparent motion of the sun. However, a lunar month is not less than 29 days or more than 30 days with a total of 354 days in a calendar year, and a solar calendar may vary from 28 to 31 days with a total of 365 days per year.

He appointed the moon for seasons: the sun knoweth his going down. - **Psalms 104:19**

Historians and archeologists reveal that all ancient civilizations used a lunar-solar calendar system, which played a role in Jewish festivals or holy holidays known as the Seven Feasts of Jehovah, which had to be celebrated on the exact date in which they were scheduled to take place. **Leviticus 23:4 -** ***These are the feasts of the Lord, even holy convocations, which ye shall proclaim in their seasons.*** More technical in nature, the Jewish calendar is based on three astronomical phenomena: (1) the rotation of the Earth around its axis (a day); (2) the revolution of the moon around the Earth (a month); and (3) the revolution of the Earth around the sun (a year).

On average, the moon revolves around the Earth in about 29½ days.

- **Rotation of the Earth**:
  The Earth orbits around the Sun, and it takes one year to go around the Sun one time. The Earth also rotates, or spins, on its axis, and it takes one day to spin around itself one time. The Earth's axis is not straight up and down, but tilted at an angle of 23.5 degrees, and the rotation is what causes the change from day to night.

- **Revolution of the Earth**:
  The movement of the Earth around the Sun in a fixed orbit is referred to as "revolving." One full orbit around the sun is one revolution. The Earth takes 365¼ days, or 1 year, to complete one revolution, which is equivalent to 12.4 lunar months. The Earth revolves around the Sun because of gravity.

The Hebrew word for day is "Yom!" **Genesis 1.5** states, *"**And God called the light Day, and the darkness he called Night. And the evening and the morning were the first day.**"* (KJV) This references the evening as being first and the morning second, as far as the order of a day is concerned. The evening is sometimes defined as the late afternoon, between 3:00 p.m. to sundown. In this case, the Hebrew calendar day begins at sundown (approximately 6:00 p.m.) and lasts for 24 hours, commencing on the next day at 5:59 p.m. and starting over with a brand new day at 6:00 p.m. An extra month is added to the Hebrew calendar every two or three years to keep the solar seasons aligned with the lunar calendar. The year in which this extra year is added is recognized as leap year. *In the <u>first month</u>, that is, the month <u>Nisan</u>, in the twelfth year of king Ahasuerus, they cast Pur, that is, the lot, before Haman from day to day, and from month to month, to the <u>twelfth month</u>, that is, the month <u>Adar</u>.* - **Ester 3:7 (KJV)**

FROM WHAT TRIBE WERE YOU BIRTHED?

MONTHS	MEANING	FARM SEASON
Nisan/Nissan or Abib/Aviv The first month March – April	The beginning of the year should start with new growth and not in the middle with everything dying to represent death. Nissan is related to the word *nissim* in Hebrew, which means "miracles." The season in which you begin to trust God using in allowing your obedience towards His every word as to be the key. And In addition, Nisan literally means, "their flight" or "break- through." This is the month to expect miracles, redemption, and deliverance.	Barley Harvest
Iyar/Iyyar or Zif/Ziv The second month April – May	The month of Iyar is about divine healing or refining (restoration) ourselves; a month of radiance or budding. Iyar/Iyyar means "rosette or blossom." Zif/Ziv means "to glow or give off light."	Barley Harvest
Sivan The third month May – June	Derived from the Akkadian word *simānu*, meaning "season or time." According to the rabbinic teachings, the Hebrew interpretation of the word Sivan means the month of vision (insight and clarity), and the power to walk thus meaning to move and accelerate in our	Wheat Harvest

http://www.yashanet.com/library/hebrew-days-and-months.html

Tammuz/Tamuz The fourth month June - July	*Tammuz* signifies "hidden – giver of the vine," which is opposite of the inspiration from which the month was actually named. *Dumuzid* (pronounced Dumu-zi) means "the son who rises; faithful or true son." *Dumuzid* was also the name of a Sumerian god of food and vegetation; and later, he was worshipped in the Mesopotamian cities of Akkad, Assyria, and Babylonia as the god of fertility. Nevertheless, this is the month in which God brought judgment on Israel for the sin of idolatry (Ezekiel 8:14-15). This marks the season or time of stirring up the evil within one's soul to confront it and to encourage self-examination, soul-searching, introspection, and reflection. It symbolizes heat, the burning flame, and fire, and it marks the beginning of summer.	Grape Harvest
Av/Ab The fifth month July - August	Based on the pronunciation of the Hebrew word "*Av*," which produces the sound *Ab*, and literally means, "father." It derives from the root word Avah, which means, "to will" or "to desire."	Olive Harvest
Elul The sixth month August - September	The word *Elul* means, "search" or "inspect." It is also called *Teshuva* for return or repentance: harvest time. This month is about returning back to God and seeking HIM with our whole heart.	Dates & Figs Harvest

FROM WHAT TRIBE WERE YOU BIRTHED?

MONTHS	MEANING	FARM SEASON
Tishri/Tishrei/Tisri or Ethanim The seventh month September - October	*Tishrei* means "to begin" and marks the beginning of autumn or fall. It symbolizes balance, justice, and DIVINE judgment. Also referenced as the month of the strong or the ancients. *Ethanim* means "ever-flowing streams."	Early Rains
Cheshvan/Heshvan or Bul The eighth month October - November	*Cheshvan* means "eight," and *Bul* means "rain, withering, increase, and produce." The spiritual meaning of the number eight is new beginnings. *Cheshvan* marks the days of Noah and the flood. After the flood, there was a new beginning: LIFE.	Plowing
Kislev/Chislev/Chisleu The ninth month November - December	As part of the word *Kislev*, there is another word (lev), which means, "heart." *Kislev* means "trust and security." Trust starts in the heart and leads to security.	Wheat & barley Sowing
Tevet/Tebeth The tenth month December - January	*Tevet* is derived from the word *tov*, which means, "good" or "goodness." The word *Tebeth* is believed to have come from an Akkadian root meaning to "sink" or "sink down" and is in line with the prevailing conditions of the seasons; a time of much wintry mix: snow, sleet, hail and rain. However, it is also a time to expect "Divine	Winter Rains

MONTHS	MEANING	FARM SEASON
Shevat/Shebat The eleventh month January - February	*Shevat*, with different vowels, means "shevet" or "tribe." The month of *Shevat* is the month for connecting to the true tzadik ("righteous one") of the generation, the Tree of Life of the generation. The themes for the month of *Shevat* are renewal and rebirth.	Almond Bloom
Adar The twelfth month February - March	The word Adar is derived from the Hebrew word "adir" which means "strength" (אדיר). Interchangeably, the word "Adar" means "strength, exalted, praised, and power." Adar is also believed to mean "to be wide" and "to be made great and honorable." It also translates to "to be exceedingly glorious, becoming glorious and magnificent."	Citrus Harvest
Adar Sheni		(Latter Rains) Intercalary Month Leap Year

FROM WHAT TRIBE WERE YOU BIRTHED?

THE FEASTS OF THE LORD	
Nisan/Nissan or Abib/Aviv	**PASSOVER** Unleavened Bread — Nisan 14 First fruits — Nisan 15-21 Passover — Nisan 18
Iyar/Iyyar or Zif/Ziv to 6 Sivan	50 days from Resurrection to Pentecost
Tishri/Tishrei/Tisri or Ethanim	**TABERNACLES** Trumpets — Tishri 1 Day of Atonement — Tishri 10 Tabernacles — Tishri 15-21

Birth Order Jacob's Sons (& Their mothers)	Star Sign - Zodiac Hebrew & Latin Based on Sacred Month Order	Sacred Month Order Hebrew & Babylonian
1- **Reuben** (Leah)	Taleh/Toleh (Aries)	Nisan/Nissan or Abib/Aviv (30 days)
2- **Simeon** (Leah)	Shur/Shaur/Shor (Taurus)	Iyar/Iyyar or Zif/Ziv (29 days)
3- **Levi** (Leah)	Teomaim/Te'amin (Gemini)	Sivan (30 days)
4- **Judah** (Leah)	Sartan (Cancer)	Tammuz/Tamuz (29 days)
5- **Dan** (Leah)	Arieh/Aryeh/Ari (Leo)	Av/Ab (30 days)
6- **Naphtali** (Bilhah)	Bethulah (Virgo)	Elul (29 days)
7- **Gad** (Zilpah)	Mozanayim (Libra)	Tishri/Tishrei/Tisri or Ethanim (30 days)
8- **Asher** (Zilpah)	Aquarav/Akrab/Akrav (Scorpio)	Cheshvan/Heshvan or Bul (29/30 days)
9- **Issachar** (Leah)	Qashot/Kasshat/Keshet (Sagittarius)	Kislev/Chislev/Chisleu (29/30 days)
10- **Zebulun** (Bilhah)	Gedi/Ghedi (Capricorn)	Tevet/Tebeth (29 days)
11- **Joseph** (Rachel)	Deli/Delli/D'li (Aquarius)	Shevat/Shebat (30 days)
12- **Benjamin** (Rachel)	Dagim (Pisces)	Adar I (28 days)
		Adar II or Adar Beit: LEAP YEAR - Resulting in an extra day: 29 days in the month for a total 366 days in the year. Takes place approximately every 4 years.

March 21 – April 20		
April 21 – May 20		
May 21 – June 20		
June 21 – July 22		
July 23 – August 22		
August 23 – September 22		
September 23 – October		
October 23 – November 22		
November 23 – December 21		
December 22 – January 19		
January 20 – February 19		
February 20 – March 20 March - April		

CHAPTER 4

*But ye are a chosen generation,
a royal priesthood, an holy nation,
a peculiar people; that ye should shew forth
the praises of him who hath called you out of
darkness into his marvellous light;*

- 1 PETER 2:9 (KJV)

FROM GENESIS TO REVELATION

There is a beginning and an end to everything, even the genealogy and generation of mankind! However, man puts more emphasis on where he is going or where he will end up, but unfortunately gives very little thought to his beginning or ancestral bloodline. God sees all, and HE pays close attention to the beginning of our existence and our ending, or our fulfillment of the purpose of our being before and after death. It all begins with HIM, the CREATOR of mankind, even the birthing of the first man and woman in the Garden of Eden! Humanity itself began with Adam and Eve, the patriarch and matriarch of civilization. Through them came the birthing of Noah, Abraham (originally named Abram), Isaac, and Yaacov/Jacob, as well as many generations to follow.

> And he (Esau) said, "Is it for this reason that he was named Jacob? For he has deceived me twice; he took my birthright, and behold, now he has taken my blessing." And he said, "Have you not reserved a blessing for me?"
> **Genesis 27:36 (CJB)**

Yaacov in Hebrew means, "holder of the heel" or "usurper in greater detail, one who seizes the power of another." Encouraged by his mother, Rebekah/Rebecca, Jacob tricked his father (Isaac) into blessing him with his oldest brother's (Esau) inheritance or birthright (see **Genesis 27:1-40**). Jacob and Esau were twins who fought incessantly, even while in their mother's womb. Esau was born first and Jacob followed while clutching or holding onto Esau's heel. When Isaac, Jacob's father, grew old and became blind, the time came for him to bless the firstborn (and oldest son) with his birthright. Not realizing that it was Jacob he was speaking to and not Esau, he bestowed upon Jacob the blessing intended for his firstborn son.

Needless to say, this only served to add more fuel to their continued sibling rivalry. Fearing for his life, Jacob fled to safety from Esau into a distant land, Paddan-aram (Haran), which was where his mother's brother Laban lived. In Akkadian, Haran means "highway, road, or caravan." Jacob not only sought refuge, but also a wife, and he ended up working for his uncle for approximately 14 years before being united with his true love. During his journey and his planned return to the homeland of his birth, Jacob wrestled with an angel of God and refused to let go until he received a blessing from the Lord. Jacob finally prevailed and was renamed Israel (Yisrael in Hebrew), meaning "he who strives or wrestles with God and prevails to having power with God and men" (Genesis 32:24-28). Prior to Jacob's name change he was characterized as, or known as being, a trickster. ***And he said, thy name shall be called no more Jacob, but Israel: for as a prince hast thou power with God and with men, and hast prevailed.*** - **Genesis 32:28**

Jacob became the patriarch of the Tribes of Israel and each one of his descendants, in turn, became the patriarch of a tribe. Subsequently, Jacob had a total of twelve sons and one daughter. In birth order, as referenced in Genesis 29:32-30:24 and 35:16-20, they were: (1) Reuben, (2) Simeon, (3) Levi, (4) Judah, (5) Dan, (6) Naphtali, (7) Gad, (8) Asher, (9) Issachar, (10) Zebulun, (11) Dinah, (12) Joseph, and (13) Benjamin. Leah, Jacob's first wife, birthed six of the twelve sons and their daughter Dinah (as referenced in Genesis 30:21). Additionally, there are references (Genesis 34:9, 16; 37:35, 46:7, 15) to the possibility of Jacob having other daughters, but they are not named.

ANN GWEN MACK

Although they are not mentioned by name and no other specifics are given, it could very well be that the references are directed at Jacob gaining more daughters after they joined in holy matrimony with his sons. Unlike today, the addition of family members through marriage was openly accepted and not viewed as step- or in-laws to denote division, and were instead considered full members of the family. Nonetheless, because the lineage of nations came through men and not through women, more importance and emphasis was put on the accomplishments of the men rather than the women. For this reason, Dinah was not considered to be a leader or head of a tribe.

FROM WHAT TRIBE WERE YOU BIRTHED?

ORDER OF BIRTH: Jacob's Children

GENESIS 29:32-35

- *And Leah conceived, and bare a son, and she called his name **Reuben (Reuven)**: for she said, Surely the LORD hath looked upon my affliction; now therefore my husband will love me.*

- *And she conceived again, and bare a son; and said, because the LORD hath heard I was hated, he hath therefore given me this son also: and she called his name **Simeon (Shimon)**.*

- *And she conceived again, and bare a son; and said, Now this time will my husband be joined unto me, because I have born him three sons: therefore was his name called **Levi**.*

- *And she conceived again, and bare a son: and she said, Now will I praise the LORD: therefore she called his name **Judah**; and left bearing.*

ANN GWEN MACK

GENESIS 30:5–13, 18-24

- *And Bilhah conceived, and bare Jacob a son. And Rachel said, God hath judged me, and hath also heard my voice, and hath given me a son: therefore called she his name **Dan**.*

- *And Bilhah, Rachel's maid conceived again, and bare Jacob a second son. And Rachel said, with great wrestlings have I wrestled with my sister, and I have prevailed: and she called his name **Naphtali**. When Leah saw that she had left bearing, she took Zilpah her maid, and gave her Jacob to wife.*

- *And Zilpah, Leah's maid bare Jacob a son. And Leah said, A troop cometh: and she called his name **Gad**.*

- *And Zilpah, Leah's maid bare Jacob a second son. And Leah said, Happy am I, for the daughters will call me blessed: and she called his name **Asher**.*

- *And Leah said, God hath given me my hire, because I have given my maiden to my husband: and she called his name **Issachar**.*

FROM WHAT TRIBE WERE YOU BIRTHED?

- *And Leah conceived again, and bare Jacob the sixth son. And Leah said, God hath endued me [with] a good dowry; now will my husband dwell with me, because I have born him six sons: and she called his name **Zebulun**.*

- *And afterwards she bare a daughter, and called her name **Dinah**.*

- *And God remembered Rachel, and God hearkened to her, and opened her womb. And she conceived, and bare a son; and said, God hath taken away my reproach: And she called his name **Joseph**; and said, The LORD shall add to me another son.*

GENESIS 35:16-18

- *And it came to pass, as her soul was in departing, (for she died) that she called his name Benoni: but his father called him **Benjamin**. And Rachel died, and was buried in the way to Ephrath, which [is] Bethlehem.*

ANN GWEN MACK

THERE IS POWER AND MEANING IN A NAME

What is a name? Simply put, a name is the grouping of several letters of the alphabet or other symbols that serve to represent the identity of a person or object in order to set it apart from the other. Tasha Cobbs's song "Break Every Chain" starts out with lyrics declaring, "There is power in the name of Jesus!" Oddly enough, people today do not seem to consider the importance of a name and should be more selective about the names they give their children! What something is called, in relation to what something truly is or is not, is the ultimate statement. However, I would argue that both are equally important. Why else would many people in the Bible have their names changed from what they were called at birth to something more in line with their God-ordained or intended purpose for being? This confirms the idea that a name can quite easily be just as much of a curse as it can be a blessing.

> *Now [in Haran] the Lord said to Abram, Go for yourself [for your own advantage] away from your country, from your relatives and your father's house, to the land that I will*

show you. And I will make of you a great nation, and I will bless you [with abundant increase of favors] and make your name famous and distinguished, and you will be a blessing [dispensing good to others]. And I will bless those who bless you [who confer prosperity or happiness upon you] and [a]curse him who curses or uses insolent language toward you; in you will all the families and kindred of the Earth be blessed [and by you they will bless themselves].
- **Genesis 12:1-3 (AMP)**

Originally named Abram (אברם) by his father, and later changed to Abraham (אברהם) by God to denote "a father of many (or a multitude of) nations," Abram went from being a fatherless man whose name meant a "father lifted up" or "exalted father," to a blessed man and father whose descendants would in turn be greatly blessed, too. The name change clearly represents a change in purpose, character and authority, thus revealing God's divine plan that would be fulfilled through Abraham and his descendants who believed in God.

This speaks to why it was important for God to change Jacob's name to "Israel," denoting greater responsibility and authority as not only a father of twelve sons—Reuben, Simeon, Levi, Judah, Dan, Naphtali, Gad, Asher, Issachar, Zebulon, Joseph, and Benjamin (for scriptural reference, please see Genesis 35:23-26; Exodus 1:1-4; 1 Chronicles 2:1-2)—but as the patriarch of the Twelve Tribes of Israel. Abram was married to Sarai when his name changed to Abraham. Her name was changed as well to Sarah, meaning "princess, a woman of high rank," or "a mother of many nations," which is in sync with her husband's status and purpose.

> *"And I will establish my covenant between me and thee and thy seed after thee in their generations for an everlasting covenant, to be a God unto thee, and to thy seed after thee."*
> *- **Genesis 17:7***

FROM WHAT TRIBE WERE YOU BIRTHED?

NAME	MOTHER	NAME MEANS	REFERENCE
Reuben	Leah	Behold (see or observe) a son, the arising son, pouring out blessings, pouring forth	Genesis 29:32
Simeon	Leah	God has heard	Genesis 29:33
Levi	Leah	Joined, joining, bound, united	Genesis 29:34
Judah	Leah	To praise	Genesis 29:35
Dan	Bilhah	Judged, judging, ruling	Genesis 30:5-6
Naphtali	Bilhah	My struggle, wrestling, sufferings at the first coming	Genesis 30:7-8
Gad	Zilpah	Troop, company, warrior, good fortune, blessings at the second coming	Genesis 30:10-11
Asher	Zilpah	Happy, blessed, blessing, the going forth of the Gospel	Genesis 30:12-13
Issachar	Leah	Hired, wages, reward, price of redemption, recompense	Genesis 30:17-18
Zebulun	Leah	Dwelling, gifts, honor of the promised seed at the first coming	Genesis 30:19-20
Joseph	Rachel	God shall add (or multiply as in double)	Genesis 30:23,24

ANN GWEN MACK

CHARACTER TRAIT & SYMBOLISM:
Order of Responsibility, Authority and Blessing

What makes us unique? Regardless of how much we try to group everyone together and label each other, we are all very different and unique. If everything indeed has its place, it would have to take into account the fact that everything good or bad has a purpose. If opposites attract, then do they not also complement one another? God does everything for a reason and a divine purpose and allows everything that takes place to occur whether we agree with it or not! HIS ways are not our ways, and our ways are not HIS, but God does have a systematic order to everything, including who we are and who we will become and for what purpose.

> *For I know the thoughts and plans that I have for you, says the Lord, thoughts and plans for welfare and peace and not for evil, to give you hope in your final outcome. Then you will call upon Me, and you will come and pray to Me, and I will hear and heed you. Then you will seek Me, inquire for, and require Me [as a vital necessity] and find Me when you search for Me with all your heart. I will be found by*

FROM WHAT TRIBE WERE YOU BIRTHED?

you, says the Lord, and I will release you from captivity and gather you from all the nations and all the places to which I have driven you, says the Lord, and I will bring you back to the place from which I caused you to be carried away captive. - **Jeremiah 29:11-14 (AMP)**

1. **Levi,** the priest (or the cleric), is Hebrew for "attached" or "joined." Levi is the third son, and three represents the TRINITY (the father, the son, and the Holy Spirit), representing royalty or priesthood. Levi was also noted for having an aggressive spirit along with his brother Simeon, but his descendants became priests and keepers of the Law.

   The Levities were teachers of the Word of God; specifically, chosen to serve in the Temple of God (YHVH), and the work of their hands were blessed (Deut. 33:8-11). You could say they were considered to be mechanical engineers with a gift for constructing, building and dismantling the Tabernacle (Neh. 1:51). The Levites did not go to war, but as demonstrated by Levi's actions in revenging his sister's honor, they were not fearful. Levi symbolizes Pisces: two fish, one pointed toward Heaven and the other toward the Ecliptic (the path of the sun). The two fish also represent the two great branches of the Church.

2. **Judah/Yehudah** in Hebrew means "praise" (or acknowledgement) as referenced in Genesis 29:35, but it also symbolizes glory, triumph, and dominion. Judah represents the Hebrew letter *Hei,* which means, "revelation, take seed, be broken." This alphabet letter is equivalent to the number five for GRACE. Based on the order of Judah's birth, he was the fourth son born to Jacob and Leah. He quickly rose in character and responsibility to be given the firstborn right of leadership and authority over the tribes.

Genesis 49:8-12 - *Judah, thou art he whom thy brethren shall praise: thy hand shall be in the neck of thine enemies; thy father's children shall bow down before thee. Judah is a lion's whelp: from the prey, my son, thou art gone up: he stooped down, he couched as a* *lion, and as an old lion; who shall rouse him up? The sceptre shall not depart from Judah, nor a lawgiver from between his feet, until Shiloh come; and unto him shall the gathering of the people be. Binding his foal unto the vine, and his ass's colt unto the choice vine; he washed his garments in wine, and his clothes in the blood of grapes: His eyes shall be red with wine, and his teeth white with milk.*

Judah was a natural born leader of the people whose descendants would be the Kings of Israel, beginning with King David and ending with *Mashiach*. *Mashiach* is Hebrew for "messiah, the anointed one." The English meaning for messiah is savior or a "hoped-for deliverer." Our Lord and Savior, Jesus Christ, was later born under the Tribe of Judah and symbolized both the lion and the sacrificial lamb. Under the sign of Cancer, he symbolizes a man who first retreats to nooks and corners like the crab, but eventually becomes as brave as a lion and rises to the occasion, reaching his destiny and purpose. **Leo, the lion: fearless and victorious**!

3. **Simeon/Shimon,** along with his brother Levi, was noted for having an aggressive spirit, but unlike Levi he was also viewed as a murderer and a criminal. However, he was actually the opposite of his brother Reuben, to the point of possessing something called *gevura or gevurah*, which is a sense of power and strength combined with a strong will for carrying out the law on the basis of a strict reward or punishment.

A fierce anger and cruel wrath resulting from unbridled *gevura* must be eliminated or it runs the risk of boiling over and becoming a weapon of violence, which can easily consume a person and anyone he or she comes in contact with! All in all, I guess you could say that Simeon and Levi were hell on wheels and two forces to be to be reckoned with!

Genesis 49:5-7 - *Simeon and Levi are indeed brothers, kindred spirits who use their swords for cruelty and violence. May*

FROM WHAT TRIBE WERE YOU BIRTHED?

I never enter their confidence; from the two of them I must part company to retain my honor. Because in their anger, they've killed men, and they've hamstrung oxen on a whim. Their anger be cursed, for they have fierce tempers. Their wrath be cursed, for they can be cruel. I will scatter their children among Jacob's descendants and spread them throughout the land of Israel. (**The VOICE**).

So, Simeon and Levi were separated and scattered among the tribes. Moses omitted Simeon, but the Simeonites did not lose their identity (**1 Chronicles 4:24-38**) and in I Chronicles 12:25, they are referenced as being mighty men of valor who are fit for war. In Revelation 7, they are identified as being selected to be part of the 144,000. Simeon stays bound in Egypt with Joseph (**Genesis 42:24**); when Joseph, having settled in Egypt, asks his brothers to bring Benjamin to him, he takes Simeon hostage to ensure that they return.

The Simeonites joined forces with the Tribe of Judah to fight against the Canaanites

(**Judges 1:3, 17**). So in turn, as their reward, the Tribe of Simeon received their inheritance within the territory of Judah (**Joshua 19:9**). Simeon symbolizes **Taurus**, the bull (or ox). Picture a bull rushing forth with mighty energy and fierce wrath, his horns set in position to push his enemies while piercing and destroying them. After Levi was elevated to priest, Simeon took on his position of Pisces on the Breastplate since their personalities were so alike. And Simeon's position was transferred over to his nephew, Ephraim (**Deuteronomy 33:17**), Joseph's second born son who was blessed by his grandfather (**Genesis 48:20**) to receive the right to the firstborn inheritance.

4. **Reuben,** the first-born ('*bechor*'), represents the powerful energy of everything that comes first. The first fruit, the first moments of the day, and the beginning of every creation all have an enormous amount of energy. However, Reuben was passed over from receiving the inheritance of the firstborn because he committed adultery with Bilhah, his father's concubine.

FROM WHAT TRIBE WERE YOU BIRTHED?

Genesis 49:3-4 - Reuben, you are my firstborn, my might, the beginning (the firstfruits) of my manly strength and vigor; [your birthright gave you] the preeminence in dignity and the preeminence in power. But unstable and boiling over like water, you shall not excel and have the preeminence [of the firstborn], because you went to your father's bed; you defiled it—he went to my couch (**AMP**)!

Due to his disobedient and defiant nature, Rueben lost his firstborn birthright, which was split between Judah and Joseph. Joseph received the double portion of the inheritance, and Judah was elevated to the position of leader of the Tribes. In addition, none of his tribe was appointed to a position of judge, king, or prophet. However, he was the only one of his brothers who wanted to spare his brother Joseph.

Genesis 42:22 - Reuben: *Didn't I tell you not to harm the boy? But you wouldn't* *listen. Now we will all pay for spilling his blood* **(The VOICE)!**

Reuben symbolizes **Aquarius**, the waterman (or water bearer); his personality was "unstable like water." As a source of untamed energy or power, he could be very explosive at any moment. If harnessed or channeled properly, his energetic presence could change worlds. But, if abused in any way, it could destroy. Water can easily erode an environment if not contained, and it can flood its surroundings. **Deuteronomy 33:6** - *Let Reuben live, and not die; and let not his men be few.*

5. **Dan** in Hebrew means "to judge," and it is the path to law and order (justice). Dan symbolizes **Libra**, the balance (scales), and is a symbol for justice. **Genesis 49:16-18** - *Dan shall judge his people, as one of the tribes of Israel. Dan shall be a serpent by the way, an adder in the path, that biteth the horse heels, so that his rider shall fall backward. I have waited for thy salvation, O Lord.*

Dan was a defender of truth who used his authority to comfort evil when necessary and did not back down or run away. Dan was as mentally strong as he was physically strong. Samson was from the Tribe of Dan **(Judges 13)**. Dan was not part of the 144,000 sealed in Revelation 7. However, as referenced by Ezekiel 48:2 and 32, a gate and land will be named after him in the millennium. **Joshua 19:47 -** *And the coast of the children of Dan went out too little for them: therefore the children of Dan went up to fight against Leshem, and took it, and smote it with the edge of the sword, and possessed it, and dwelt therein, and called Leshem, Dan, after the name of Dan their father.*

6. **Naphtali** is like a "deer running free" and breaking out of the status quo. A deer is a swift runner, independent and free. Naphtali had a way with words and an ability to "deliver words of beauty." **Genesis 49:21 -** *Naphtali is a wild doe that gives birth to beautiful fawns.* He symbolizes Virgo, the virgin.

7. **Gad**, the prophet and seer (the King's seer) is the warrior archetype who is also known as the gracious one. Expanding on the justice of Dan, Gad is ready to fight for his beliefs and the rights of others. The warrior is necessary to both defend our cherished values and to protect our freedoms. Gad was the raiding band, the tribe most gifted with the art of the bow. He symbolizes **Sagittarius**, the archer, and is Hebrew for "what good fortune!" **Genesis 49:19** - *Gad, a troop shall overcome him: but he shall overcome at the last*. Gad was ready to fight for his beliefs and triumphed over adversity. He was a leader of the people and did for Israel what the Lord considered fair and honorable (**Deuteronomy 33:21**).

In addition, he was a prophet and King David's seer (**1 Samuel 22:5**), telling David to build an altar for the Lord at the Temple Mount in Jerusalem (**2 Samuel 24**). *Gad: "Blessed is he who makes Gad large. Gad roams like a lion, tears off an arm, rips open a skull. He took one look and grabbed the best place for himself, the portion just made for someone in* *charge. He took his place at the head, carried out God's right ways and his rules for life in Israel."* - **Deuternomy 33:20-21 (MSG)**

8. **Asher**, the prosperous one, is a Hebrew name derived from the word *ashar*, which means "blessed, happy, prosper, straight, honest, go, guide, lead, and relieve." Asher is the dimension of blessing beyond the norm – to be given more than what is necessary for survival (abundant).

Genesis 49:20 - *Asher's food [supply] shall be rich and fat, and he shall yield and deliver royal delights.* Asher is a representation of not just getting what you need, but also enjoying it.

Deuteronomy 33:24-25 - *About the tribe of Asher he said, "The people of Asher are the most blessed of the sons of Israel. May they be the Israelites' favorite tribe and wash their feet in olive oil. May the locks and bolts of your gates be made of iron and copper. May your strength last as long as you live.* **(GW)**

9. **Issachar** translates to "there is a reward." The tribe noted for being gifted scholars dedicated to learning, intellectual growth, and studying. They possess great insight (clarity) and wisdom, which is the foundation for any success.

Genesis 49:14 - *Issachar is a strong-boned donkey crouching down between the sheepfolds. And he saw that rest was good and that the land was pleasant; and he bowed his shoulder to bear his burdens and became a servant to tribute subjected to forced labor.* Issachar symbolizes **Cancer**, the crab or crayfish, which is linked to a donkey or an ass. Within the constellation of the stars that form Cancer, there are two stars known as the *Aselli* (Latin plural for asses or donkeys).

Each star represents the **North** Asellus (γ, gamma Asellus borealis) and the **South** Asellus (δ, delta, Asellus Australis). *Asellus* is singular in Latin of a little ass or donkey, which is situated in the body of the crab. Another important star that sits in the center formation of the Cancer constellation is called the Beehive Cluster or the *Praesepe*, which is Latin for "manger." The manger represents "a trough in which two donkeys (one on the north side and one on the east side) are being fed." According to ancient Greek philosophy, Cancer is the gateway through which souls descend from heaven to the bodies of the newly born. The trough represents the manger that Christ was placed in when HE was born, and the donkeys represent those present during HIS birth.

10. **Zebulun**, the business man, is derived from the Hebrew name *Zebuwluwn*, which means "dwelling" or "habitation." Zebulun would dwell by the seashore. He symbolizes **Capricorn**, the Sea Goat. **Genesis 49:13 -** ***Zebulun shall dwell at the haven of the sea; and he shall be for an haven of ships; and his border shall be unto Zidon***. As merchant and businessmen, Zebulun and Issachar complemented each other by forging a partnership that supported the endeavor of teaching (education and scholarship).

His role or area of authority and territory was over the marketplace and their mission was to redeem the Divine sparks within the material world otherwise known as the 'secret treasure hidden in the sand' (**Deuteronomy 33:19**).

11. **Joseph** is the element of suffering in life. Yet, not only does he survive, he thrives. He achieves greatness through his challenges. He overcomes all adversaries and becomes a great leader, saving his entire generation from famine. Despite the corruption around him, he maintains his spiritual integrity and becomes fruitful.

***Genesis 49:22-26** - Joseph is a fruitful bough, even a fruitful bough by a well; whose branches run over the wall: The archers have sorely grieved him, and shot at him, and hated him: But his bow abode in strength, and the arms of his hands were made strong by the hands of the mighty God of Jacob; (from thence is the shepherd, the stone of Israel:) Even by the God of thy father, who shall help thee; and by the Almighty, who* *shall bless thee with blessings of heaven above, blessings of the deep that lieth under, blessings of the breasts, and of the womb: The blessings of thy father have prevailed above the blessings of my progenitors unto the utmost bound of the everlasting hills: they shall be on the head of Joseph, and on the crown of the head of him that was separate from his brethren.*

Joseph's brothers were jealous of him because he was their father's favorite, not to mention he was a dreamer.

Genesis 37:5-8 - *Joseph had a dream, and when he told it to his brothers, they hated him all the more. He said to them, "Listen to this dream I had: We were binding sheaves of grain out in the field when suddenly my sheaf rose and stood upright, while your sheaves gathered around mine and bowed down to it." His brothers said to him, "Do you intend to reign over us? Will you actually rule us?" And they hated him all the more* *because of his dream and what he had said* **(NIV).**

So his brothers sold him into slavery and convinced their father that Joseph was dead. But this was all part of God's plan. Joseph was brought into Egypt, where his ability to interpret visions earned him a place in the Pharaoh's court, paving the way for his family's later settlement in Egypt. Joseph symbolizes Gemini, the twins. In this case he represents the double blessing of Ephraim and Manasseh, who were adopted and by Jacob, their grandfather. **Genesis 48:5 -** *And now thy two sons, Ephraim and Manasseh, which were born unto thee in the land of Egypt before I came unto thee into Egypt, are mine; as Reuben and Simeon, they shall be mine.* *The powerful light that emerges from darkness (the peril of his suffering) in Joseph divides into two dimensions – his two sons:*

- **Menashe/Manasseh** means "to forget." *And Joseph called the name of the firstborn Manasseh: For God, said he,* *hath made me forget all my toil, and all my father's house* (**Genesis 41:52**). Manasseh assumed his father's position under Gemini as one of the Twelve Tribes of Israel.

- **Ephraim** means "double fruitfulness." *And the name of the second called he Ephraim: For God hath caused me to be fruitful in the land of my affliction* (**Genesis 41:52**). Ephraim received the firstborn blessing. *And he (Jacob) blessed them that day, saying, in thee shall Israel bless, saying, God make thee as Ephraim and as Manasseh: and he set Ephraim before Manasseh* (**Genesis 48:20**). *His glory is like the firstling of his bullock, and his horns are like the horns of unicorns: with them he shall push the people together to the ends of the Earth: and they are the ten thousands of Ephraim, and they are the thousands of Manasseh* (**Deuteronomy 33:17**).

12. **Benjamin,** the ravenous consumer. In Hebrew his name is Binyamin, and in

Greek it is spelled *Beniamín*; both mean "son of the south" or "son of the right hand". Benjamin was a ravenous wolf who ate the spoils of victory. **Genesis 49:27 - *Benjamin shall ravin as a wolf: in the morning he shall devour the prey, and at night he shall divide the spoil.*** He is hungry for the Divine sparks that are in all of existence, and like a "ravenous wolf," Benjamin recognizes that his mission is to passionately seek out the divine energy embedded in matter, and to devour it, consume, and elevate it. (Of all of the tribes of Israel, Benjamin was the only tribe that was born in the land of Israel). ***And of Benjamin he said, The beloved of the LORD shall dwell in safety by him; [and the LORD] shall cover him all the day long, and he shall dwell between his shoulders* (Deuteronomy 33:12).** Here we explicitly see that Benjamin symbolizes both trust (safety) and rest (dwell).

All these are the TWELVE TRIBES OF ISRAEL!

FROM WHAT TRIBE WERE YOU BIRTHED?

BIBLICAL CALENDAR ORDER

Birth Order Sons of Jacob (& Their mothers)	MONTHS		Star Sign – Symbol Based on Birth Order and Character/Purpose
	Hebrew/Babylonian Transliteration	Original Sacred Order	
4 - **Judah** (Leah)	Nisan or Abib/Aviv (30 days)	**March 21** – April 20	Leo, the Lion
2 - **Simeon** (Leah)	Iyar/Iyyar or Zif/Ziv (29 days)	**April 21** – May 20	Taurus, the Bull/Ox
3 - **Levi** (Leah)	Sivan (30 days)	**May 21** – June 20	Pisces, the Fish
1 - **Reuben** (Leah)	Tammuz (29 days)	**June 21** – July 22	Aquarius, the Water Bearer or Water Man
5 - **Dan** (Leah)	Av/Ab (30 days)	**July 23** – August 22	Libra, the Scales or Eagle
6 - **Naphtali** (Bilhah)	Elul (29 days)	**August 23** – September 22	Virgo, the Virgin Woman
7 - **Gad** (Zilpah)	Tishri/Tishrei or Ethanim (30 days)	**September 23** – October	Sagittarius, the Archer
8 - **Asher** (Zilpah)	Cheshvan/Heshvan or Bul (29 or 30 days)	**October 23** – November 22	Scorpio, the Scorpion
9 - **Issachar** (Leah)	Kislev/Chislev/Chisleu (29 or 30 days)	**November 23** – December 21	Cancer, the Crab (Crayfish)
10 - **Zebulun** (Bilhah)	Tevet/Tebeth (29 days)	**December 22** – January 19	Capricorn, the Sea Goat
11 - **Joseph** (Rachel)	Shevat/Shebat (30 days)	**January 20** - February 19	Gemini, the Twins (Double portion or blessing)
12 - **Benjamin** (Rachel)	Adar I (28 days)	**February 20** – March 20 March - April	Aries, the Ram
13 - in leap years	Adar II or Adar Beit: LEAP YEAR - Resulting in an extra day; 29 days in the month for a total 366 days in the year. Takes place approximately every 4 years		

ANN GWEN MACK

And the children of Israel
were fruitful, and increased abundantly,
and multiplied, and waxed exceeding mighty;
and the land was filled with them.
- Exodus 1:7 (KJV)

THE TWELVE TRIBES OF ISRAEL

The Hebrew word for "tribe," as used in this context, is *Mateh,* and it is interchangeable with the word *Shevet*. In Hebrew, *Mateh* means "staff" or "rod" and denotes leadership or ruler-ship. Both words can also mean branch or offshoot. Thus, the tribe is a branch or offshoot from the main trunk. The Son of God, Jesus Christ, is the true vine that extends from the root of God, the father (see John 15). And we, God's children, are the branches that extend from the true vine.

Each person is expected to serve his or her intended purpose as a functioning part of the whole and work together in unison (as one body) in order to carry out the mission, goals, and objectives of GOD, the creator of us all. *For as we have many members in one body, and all members have not the same office: So we, [being] many, are one body in Christ, and every one members one of another.* (**Romans 12:4-5**)

As a rule, it was customary for all firstborn sons of Israel to serve as their family's priest. However, when Moses went to Mount Sinai to seek the LORD and to receive the Ten Commandments from God, the Israelites whom Moses had just led out of Egypt were worried that he would not return, and they grew impatient. To appease them, Aaron told the Israelites to give him their gold earrings and other things made of gold so he could build a god for them to worship.

This was an act of sin and an abomination against God, and it set a number of other events in motion. *And it came to pass, as soon as he came nigh unto the camp, that he saw the calf, and the dancing: and Moses' anger waxed hot, and he cast the tables out of his hands, and brake them beneath the mount* (**Exodus 32.19**). *He took the calf they had made and burned it in the fire, and ground it to powder and scattered it on the water and made the Israelites drink it* (**Exodus 32.20**).

Moses's reaction put him in the Lord's hot seat! Although he led the Israelites out of Egypt to Canaan, his disobedience banned him from the Promised Land. In other words, the Levites, who were descendants of Moses and Aaron, did not receive a territory in the Promised Land as the other tribes did. Instead, they became priests and had several cities scattered throughout all of Israel amongst the other tribes. **Joshua 18:7 (KJV) -** *But the Levites have no part among you; for the priesthood of the LORD [is] their inheritance: and Gad, and Reuben, and half the tribe of Manasseh, have received their inheritance beyond Jordan on the east, which Moses the servant of the LORD gave them.*

To reiterate, upon the death of a father, it was customary for the firstborn son to become the head of the home and receive a double portion of his share of the inheritance as a right. *If a man have two wives, one beloved, and another hated, and they have born him children, [both] the beloved and the hated; and [if] the firstborn son be hers that was hated: Then it shall be, when he maketh his sons to inherit [that] which he hath, [that] he may not make the son of the beloved firstborn before the son of the hated, [which is indeed] the firstborn: But he shall acknowledge the son of the hated [for] the firstborn, by giving him a double portion of all that he hath: for he [is] the beginning of his strength; the right of the firstborn [is] his.* (**Deuteronomy 21:15-17**)

In addition to Levi not receiving a territory, Joseph did not receive a tribe either. He was governor over all the land of Egypt (Genesis 45:26). However, his inheritance was handed down to his two sons, Ephraim and Manasseh. Essentially, Jacob adopted them (Genesis 48:3-6). Despite Joseph's suffering, he had a forgiving and humble spirit; *he placed his father and his brethren, and gave them a possession in the land of Egypt, in the best of the land, in the land of Rameses, as Pharaoh had commanded. And Joseph nourished his father, and his brethren, and all his father's household, with bread, according to [their] families* (**Genesis 47:11-12**)! As referenced in Joshua, this accounts for the renaming of the tribes as Reuben, Simeon, Judah, Dan, Naphtali, Gad, Asher, Issachar, Zebulun, Ephraim, Manasseh and Benjamin.

In the wilderness, the tribes were encamped around the Tabernacle in specific formation (order) as instructed by God. *Every man of the children of Israel shall pitch by his own standard, with the ensign of their father's house: far off about the tabernacle of the congregation shall they pitch* (**Numbers 2:2**). Marching forward, the tribes were to proceed in that same formulation.

First, the camp led by Judah and his tribe was positioned in the East towards the rising of the sun. Second, the camp led by Rueben and his tribe was positioned in the south. *Then the tabernacle of the congregation shall set forward with the camp of the Levites in the midst of the camp: as they encamp, so shall they set forward, every man in his place by their standards* (**Numbers 2:17**). The third camp or Tribe of Ephraim (youngest son of Joseph) was positioned in the west. The fourth and last camp led by Dan and his tribe was positioned in the north as instructed to guard the Tabernacle from behind. *And the children of Israel did according to all that the LORD commanded Moses: so they pitched by their standards, and so they set forward, every one after their families,*

FROM WHAT TRIBE WERE YOU BIRTHED?

according to the house of their fathers **(Numbers 2:34).**

The precious gemstones on the Breastplate are presented in the same order as the encampment of the tribes and marching formation. This is different from the order in which they were presented on the shoulder stone (Sardonyx) of the High Priest Ephod. As confirmed by The Bible Educator, Volume 1, page 347, the Sardonyx was on the shoulder of the Ephod. The names of the six youngest sons were engraved on the stone on the left, and the names of the six eldest sons were engraved on the stone on the right shoulder.

Zarah means "East Brightness"; Judah is the brightest position in the East!

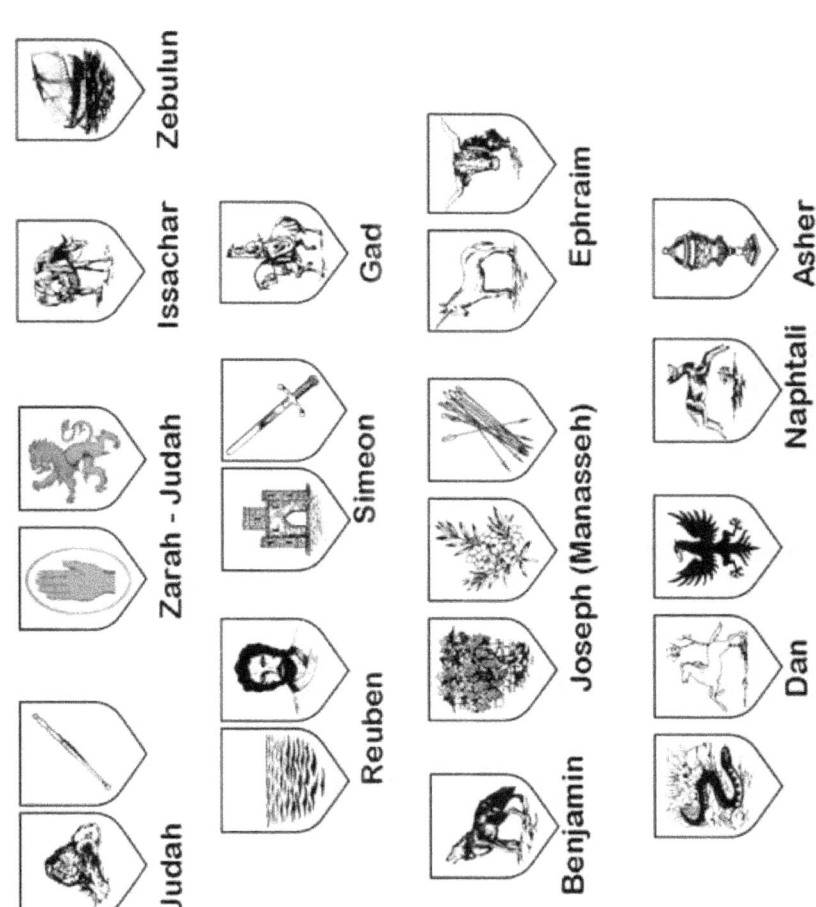

FROM WHAT TRIBE WERE YOU BIRTHED?

THE TWELVE TRIBES OF ISRAEL POSITION AND CAMP ORDER			
CAMP JUDAH	4 - Judah	Leo, the Lion	The Lion of the tribe of Judah: the consummated triumph of the redeemer in the end.
Group 1	9 - Issachar	**Cancer,** the Crab	The crab: assembled together; the redeemer's possessions held fast.
East	10 - Zebulun	**Capricorn,** the Sea Goat	The sea or kid goat: the goat of atonement slain for the redeemed.
CAMP REUBEN	1 - Reuben	**Aquarius,** the Water Man	The water bearer or water-man: the living waters of blessing poured forth for the redeemed.
Group 2	2 – Simeon	**Pisces,** the Fish	The fishes: the multitudes who will follow; the blessings of the redeemed.
South	7 - Gad	**Sagittarius,** the Archer	The archer: the gracious one; the redeemer's triumph.
CENTER	3 - LEVI	**TABERNACLE**	**MOSES, AARON, GERSHON, KOHATH, & MERARI**
CAMP EPHRAIM	11 – Joseph		
Group 3	Ephraim	**Taurus,** the Bull (Ox)	The bull or ox: the congregation of the judge; the coming judge of all the Earth.
West	Manasseh	**Gemini,** the Twins	The twins: two natures; the reign of the prince of peace.
	12 - Benjamin	**Aries,** the Ram	The ram or lamb: wounded and slain, the blessings of the redeemed consummated.
CAMP DAN	5 - Dan	**Libra,** the Scales or Eagle	The scales or eagle: the price deficient balanced by the price that covers.
Group 4	8 - Asher	**Scorpio,** the Scorpion	The scorpion: the attack of the enemy; the redeemer's conflict.
	6 - Naphtali	Virgo, the Virgin Woman	The virgin man holding a branch and an ear of

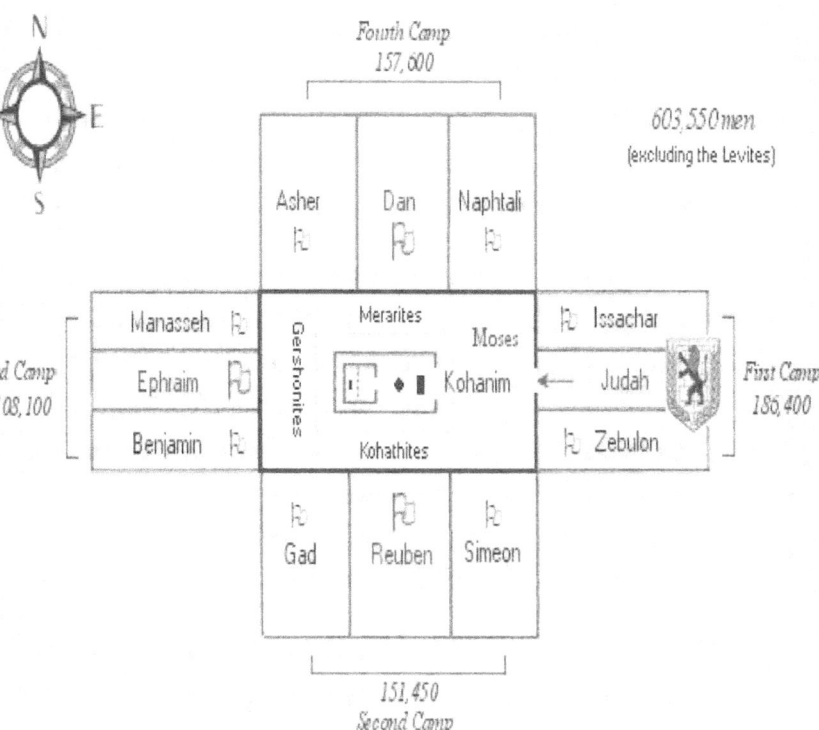

LAND DISTRIBUTION

For distribution of the Promised Land among the Twelve Tribes, see **Joshua 13–19 and 21:4-8.** This is when the Levites were scattered in several cities among the Twelve Tribes in four divisions: (1) the **Kohathite** descendants of Aaron from Judah, Simeon, and Benjamin; (2) the other **Kohathite** clans from Ephraim, Dan, and half Manasseh; (3) the **Gershonite** clans from Issachar, Asher, Naphtali, and half Manasseh; and (4) the **Merarite** clans from Rueben, Gad, and Zebulun. In more detail, additional information about the land distribution is referenced in **Ezekiel 48:1-29**.

And I will give unto thee, and to thy seed after thee, the land wherein thou art a stranger, all the land of Canaan, for an everlasting possession; and I will be their God. And God said unto Abraham, Thou shalt keep my covenant therefore, thou, and thy seed after thee in their generations. **- Genesis 17:8 -9**

Moses, Aaron, and Miriam were the leaders of the Children of Israel, and they belonged to the Tribe of Levi. The Levites were the only tribe set apart on behalf of the LORD to provide support for Aaron and his sons and aid them in performing their duties as required by the various sacred services surrounding the Tabernacle.

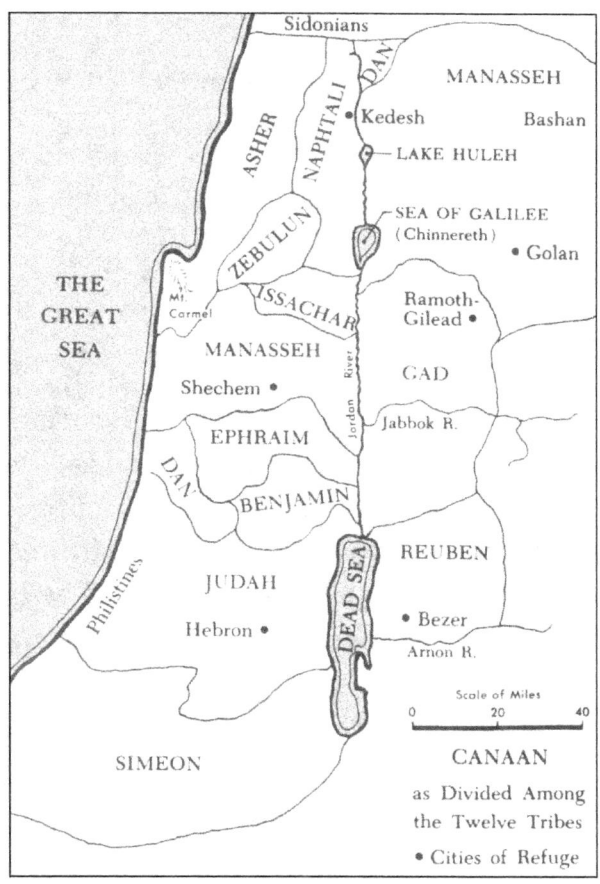

POSITION [along with the Twelve Tribes of Israel]

- Merari (Merarites): Mahli and Mushi – positioned in the **NORTH**

- Gershon (Gerhonites): Libni and Shimi – positioned in the **WEST**

- Kohath (Kohathites): Amram, Izhar, Hebron and Uzziel – positioned in the **SOUTH**

- Moses and his family, and Aaron and his family (sons: Eleazar and Ithamar) – positioned in the **EAST**

The men did the work faithfully. Their overseers were Jahath and Obadiah, Levites of the sons of Merari, and Zechariah and Meshullam, of the sons of the Kohathites. The Levites—all who were skillful with instruments of music—also had oversight of the burden bearers and all who did work in any kind of service; and some of the Levites were scribes, officials, and gatekeepers. **- 2 Chronicles 34:12-13 (AMP)**

CHAPTER 5

*And these [are] the garments
which they shall make;
a breastplate, and an ephod, and a robe,
and a broidered coat, a mitre, and a girdle:
and they shall make holy garments
for Aaron thy brother, and his sons,
that he may minister
unto me in the priest's office.*

- **EXODUS 28:4 (KJV)**

FROM WHAT TRIBE WERE YOU BIRTHED?

THE BREASTPLATE (HOSHEN) OF AARON

Moses and Aaron were descendants of the Tribe of Levi. Aaron and his sons, Nadab, Abihu, Eleazar and Ithamar were set apart, and they gladly committed themselves to serving the LORD in order to answer their calling as priests. ***Then Moses stood in the gate of the camp, and said, "Who [is] on the LORD'S side? [let him come] unto me." And all the sons of Levi gathered themselves together unto him*** **(Exodus 32:26).**

Aaron was appointed the leader of the Levitical tribe, and God gave Moses specific instructions concerning the construction of the holy garments that Aaron, the High Priest, was to wear. These very important and consecrated garments were: a girdle (white undergarments); an inner robe with long sleeves that reached the ankles; a blue short-sleeved outer robe that reached the calves; a holy vest with front and back panels (also called an ephod), which was joined at the shoulders and reached halfway down the thighs; a waistband or sash to hold the front and back panels of the holy vest close to him; a breastplate for the outside of the vest and a white turban called the mitre. Special garments were made for Aaron's sons, too.

The ephod, as referenced above, refers to the holy vest that was made of fine linen beautifully embroidered with gold, blue, purple, and scarlet threads. The front and back panels of the ephod were joined at the shoulders by two shoulder pieces. Two gemstones, Sardonyx, were engraved with the names of the twelve sons of Jacob that represented the Twelve Tribes of Israel, six names on each stone in the order of their birth. The first six and oldest sons were on the right shoulder and the last six and youngest were on the left shoulder.

As an important part of the garment, the Breastplate is referenced by other names, like the Breastplate of Aaron, the Breastplate of Judgment, and the Breastplate of Decision. It was a foot long and contained a foot-wide pouch inlaid or adorned with twelve precious gemstones (three rows across and four columns down) with two separate large stones on the right and left called the *Urim*, representing light and excellence, and the *Thummin*, representing perfection and completion. Each was engraved with the names of the sons (or descendants) of Jacob, but also represented the Twelve Tribes of Israel and was to be worn over the heart of the High Priest, Aaron, when he entered the temple in prayer. God specifically selected each gemstone, which speaks to the character, personality, and purpose of each individual tribe. It should be noted, however, that there is a difference between the Twelve Sons of Israel and the Twelve Tribes of Israel.

Identification of the gemstones, including their order, varies from one translation of the Bible to another, thus making it somewhat difficult to narrow down the exact certainty of the stones as God named them. However, the arrangement of the gemstones on the Breastplate should coincide with the order of their importance (position and leadership) as God deemed. The arranged order of the precious stones on the Breastplate is entirely different from the birth order of Israel's (Jacob's) children; however, it coincides with the encampment and marching order of those that surrounded the Tabernacle. After much research, I found that it was necessary to use an Orthodox Jewish Bible (OJB) or Hebrew Bible for accuracy, as opposed to the King James Bible, and the Book of Exodus (Shemot) 28:17-20, as referenced below in comparison to the New Living Translation (NLT):

[17]And thou shalt set in it settings of even (stone), four rows of gemstones: the first row shall be an Odem - Sard/Sardius is **Carnelian**; a Pit'dah - **Peridot,** a form of Olivine; Barekes/smaragdos - **Malachite**: this shall be the first row. [18]And the second row shall be Nofech - **Turquoise**, Sapphire – **Lapis Lazuli**, and Yahalom - **Rock Crystal Quartz**. [19]And the third row a Leshem/Ligure - **Zircon**, Shevo/Shebo - **Hematite**, and Achlamah - **Amethyst**. [20]And the fourth row Tarshish (chrysolithus/chrysolite or beryl) – **Citrine** or Cat's Eye, Shoham - **Serpentine**, and Yashfeh - **Bloodstone Jasper**; they shall be set in zahav in their settings.

---

[1] The chemical composition for "citrine" is SiO_2. The color of citrine is due to trace amounts (approximately 40 parts per million) of iron ($Fe3+$) impurities in the crystal structure of quartz. The difference between citrine and amethyst is from the oxidation state of the iron impurities present in the quartz.

FROM WHAT TRIBE WERE YOU BIRTHED?

[*Please note*: These gemstones were positioned on the breastplate from right to left with the first stone in the first row from the right being **Carnelian**.]

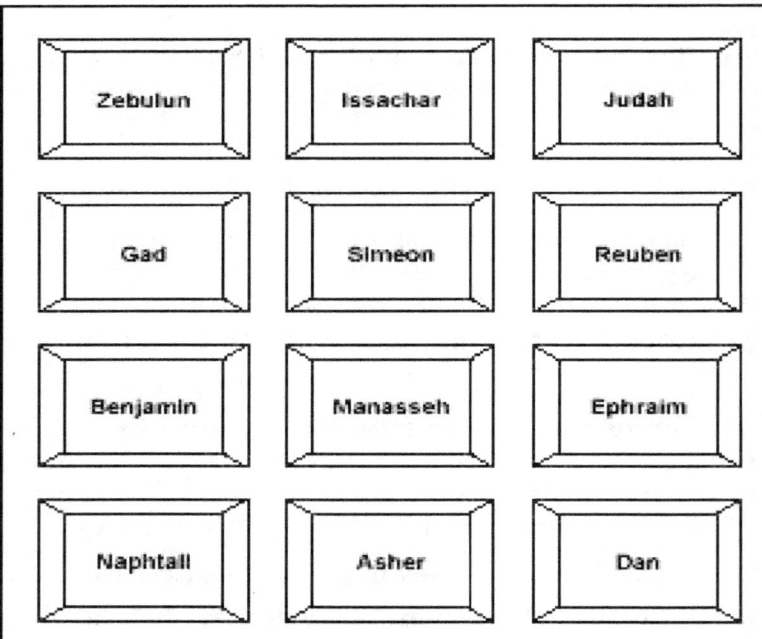

ANN GWEN MACK

THE HIGH PRIEST'S BREASTPLATE

ROW	TRIBE	HEBREW	MEANING	GREEK/LATIN	MODERN NAME
1	**Judah**	Odem	Red earth or flesh colored stone; symbolizes "BLOOD"	sardius, sardion, sard	**Carnelian**, red jasper – symbolizes KING.
	Issachar	Pitdaw or Pit'dah	Prize, reward, redemption	topazius, topazion, topaz	**Peridot**, a form of Olivine
	Zebulon	Bārekath	To glisten or shining thing	Zmaragdus, smaragdos-emerald green gem	**Malachite**,green feldspar
2	**Reuben**	Nöphek (carbuncle)	Shining stone; sparkling like lightning, or morning star	mafkat (Egyptian)	**Turquoise** Chrysocolla, the color of blue-green water and the blue skies
	Simeon	Sappîr Sappiyr		sappheiros	**Lapis Lazuli**, dark blue with silver or white specks
	Gad	Shebuw Shebo	To flame (flashing), split into tongues	achates	**Hematite**, silvery grey-black
3	**Ephraim**	Leshem Ligure	Crushing stone; dedicated to God	ligurion, ligyrion, Ligyrius (ligure)	**Zircon**, mustard brown
	Manasseh	Yahalôm Halam	Tough stone: to smile, hammer, strike down, overcome	iaspis	**Rock Crystal** *Quartz*
	Benjamin	Achlamáh/ Ahlamah	Dream stone: not drunken	Amethustos, ametustos, amethystos, Amethistus	**Amethyst**, purple

FROM WHAT TRIBE WERE YOU BIRTHED?

THE HIGH PRIEST'S BREASTPLATE

ROW	TRIBE	HEBREW	MEANING	GREEK/LATIN	MOFRT'N NSMR
4	**Dan**	Shôham	Fire or splendor; serpent fire	Berullion, bhrullos, berylos (beryl)	**Serpentine**, leek-green
	Asher	Tarshish	Spiritual love of truth	chrusolithos, chrysolithos, Chrysolitus (chrysolite)	**Citrine**[3], golden yellow or Cat's Eye, also golden yellow
	Naphtali	Yâshephêh Yashephdeh	Polished thing	iaspis	**Bloodstone**, green jasper with red specks

Levi   Sardonyx/Sardonux: Carnelian (Sard) and Alabaster (Onyx)], and the Urim & the Thummin
Joseph   Amethyst: purple, the color of royalty.

CHAPTER 6

*Wisdom is the principal thing,
therefore get wisdom and with all thy
getting get understanding.
Exalt her, and she shall promote thee:
she shall bring thee to honour,
when thou dost embrace her.*

- PROVERBS 4:7-8 (KJV)

CONCLUSION: THE IMPORTANCE OF KNOWING WHO YOU ARE

EVERYTHING in life, as created and inspired by God, is connected. God is the ultimate master of the universe, and ***we know that all things work together for good to them that love God, to them who are the called according to [his] purpose*** (Romans 8:28). In the beginning of all creation (heaven, Earth, and civilization), there was the Word. The Word was with God because the Word was and is God. And the Word was made flesh, became the Living Word who dwelt among us. We beheld HIS Glory—the glory of the only begotten son of the Father—full of grace and truth. Nothing happens without HIS permission or HIS blessing, from the beginning to the end!

How often have you heard parents who have more than one child say they do not treat or love their children differently? As one of five children, I can honestly say that I noticed a big difference in the way my parents responded to me while I was growing up, compared to how they responded to my siblings. As human beings, who are more influenced by our flesh, we tend to view each other on the basis of our subjective thoughts, hang-ups, and misguided perceptions. Instead of seeing one another with compassion, as having potential beyond what we are in life, we unjustly condemn one another. However, God sees us in a different light, not only considering our flaws, but also concerning our potential, based on who we were created to be as we attempt to reach our divine destiny!

Have you considered the difference between Jacob's blessing (Genesis 49) as it was bestowed upon his children, and God's blessing through HIS servant, Moses, the prophet, as directed towards the Twelve Tribes of Israel (**Deuteronomy 33**)? God has been encouraging me and teaching me to utilize the art of discernment in every aspect of my life, and for years HE has been giving me answers and insight into my true identity. Just as my deliverance is continuous, the pieces to a divine puzzle have been unraveling very slowly for me for a long time.

God's approach can be subtle and rather abrupt in HIS attempt to get your attention. HIS timing is strategic, and it is done systematically to bring about correction, understanding, wisdom, and knowledge. Each and every life experience (good, bad, or indifferent), including every God-given assignment, has recreated an everlasting bond between my Heavenly Father and me. Thoughts and memories have allowed me to see myself as HE sees me, to get me to acknowledge and to accept that there is more to me than what this world has to offer, and to have confidence in fulfilling my calling!

> ***All** scripture [is] given by inspiration of God, and [is] profitable for doctrine, for reproof, for correction, for instruction in righteousness: that the man of God may be perfect, throughly furnished unto all good works.*
>
> *- 2 Timothy 3:17 (KJV)*

Initially, upon receiving this assignment, I had no idea of where to start. The more God revealed the nature of HIS plan and objective to me, the more overwhelmed I became by having to process HIS knowledge and wisdom. My excitement grew from being intrigued to being frustrated, then procrastinating, and back to being intrigued again! Then came doubting my ability to effectively communicate the information that was being directed to me, as if something or someone was attempting to prevent God's message from getting through. One deadline after the other came and went along with my confidence in grasping all of what I needed to learn and share in a timely manner. But, on the morning of December 20, 2014, five days after my target date, God reassured me why I had been chosen to receive this inspiration.

When we claim God as our Father, it is the Holy Spirit who testifies with us that we truly are God's children. If we're God's children, then we're His heirs and fellow-heirs with Christ, provided that we share in the struggles and suffering which Christ also had in living a righteous life in a sinful world. If we share in His sufferings, we will also share in His glory **(Romans 8:16-17)**

God is a God of order, and that cannot be said enough! HE is very specific, if not particular, about the expectation of HIS plan, including who we were created to be with HIS appointed timing. Some of us are able to see beyond the surface of the natural to tap into the supernatural that flows *with* God and not against HIM, but we all have a role in HIS master plan. HE knows us better than we know ourselves because HE created us specifically for HIMSELF. HE maps out each event in our lives, knowing the beginning and the ending, including all of the mistakes we make in between. Then HE sits back quietly, but never too far away, while allowing everything to play out as we go through the process of obtaining HIS wisdom, HIS knowledge and HIS understanding on the road to spiritual maturity. HE teaches us the way, the truth and the life **(John 14:6)** through wisdom in the name of Jesus Christ, and leads us towards the right paths **(Proverbs 4:11)**. However, it is up to us to stay on the straight and narrow **(Matthew 7:14)** pathway. We should never look for shortcuts, even though many do as they stumble and fall along the way to destruction.

ANN GWEN MACK

As children of God, we all are created with a purpose and for a purpose, and we are given free will to make our own choices to follow HIM in pursuit of our destiny. Although we are sinners, born into iniquity, God will not give up on us or abandon us. In fact, unlike man, HE never gives up on us, and as long as we are willing HE is forever able and willing to see us through! In spite of our failures, God loves us and sees our value and worth. The LORD has a plan for each individual's life, and that plan includes salvation and total obedience to HIS word.

FROM WHAT TRIBE WERE YOU BIRTHED?

SO, WHO AM I?

I am the called generation! ***Who hath wrought and done [it], calling the generations from the beginning? I the LORD, the first, and with the last; I [am] HE*** (Isaiah 41:4). If you are anything like me, you are inquisitive and full of questions, needing to know the what, why, and how! Astonishingly, God has indulged me every step of the way! Because, for me, knowing is half the battle, regardless of whether I can control or change the outcome. Ironically, after realizing my difficulty for fitting in, I started to notice I was adapting and becoming more and more comfortable with not fitting in.

To my surprise, I could hear God encouraging me to "come out from among them to be ye separate (2 Corinthians 6:17)" and to be set apart. In fact, many viewed and accused me of being antisocial without having a clue of my destiny! Attempting to understand more about myself and my strong inexplicable urge to be different and fight for righteousness—not only for myself, but for others as well—I wanted so desperately to know from which side of my immediate family I took after in this regard. Though I needed to be more informed about the roots of my heritage, I could not consult my grandparents on either of my parent's side because they were deceased.

Since the day of my mother's passing on August 17, 2014, I started to feel more lost. However, I was also more driven than ever to push forward beyond my pain and suffering. Slowly, God started to direct me to the answer of my most important questions: "Who AM I?" and "Who was I created to be?" HALLELUJA!

And the Lord direct your hearts onto the love of God, and into the patient waiting for Christ.

- 2 Thessalonians 3:5

First, my name is Ann, which means much grace, or, more specifically in accordance to many Hebrew references, "God has favored me!" The closest to the origin of my name in the Bible is Hannah in Hebrew. I was born in the month of September on the 23rd day.

FROM WHAT TRIBE WERE YOU BIRTHED?

If you were to add two and three which is five, the result spiritually represents GRACE. Prior to the Jews being exiled from Judah to Babylonia in 586 BC, September was known as **Ethanim,** meaning month of the gifts or vintage offerings and later renamed Tishrei, Tishri, or Tisri, which means, "to begin." Overall, symbolizing a steady flow or forever flowing, September contains the most holy days that are referred to today as the "High Holy Days." God originally intended September to be the seventh month; and, the spiritual meaning of seven is "full," "fullness," "completion," or "divine perfection." Gad was the seventh child born to Jacob, and I hail from the tribe of Gad.

> *Gad will be attacked by a band of raiders, but he will strike back at their heels.*
>
> **- Genesis 49:19**

THE TRIBE OF GAD

- Gad, a prophet and seer, was appointed to guard the south side of the Tabernacle as part of the Camp of Rueben. Gad means, "fortunate" or "good fortunate."

  In **Genesis 30:11,** *Leah said, a troop cometh. So, she called his name Gad.* According to other references, Gad was known as a courageous soldier or warrior. The Gad Tribe symbolized courage and triumphed in adversity. Gad had seven sons: Ziphion (Zephon), Haggi, Shuni, Ezbon, Eri, Arodi, and Areli (Genesis 46:16, Numbers 26:15-17).

- Gad's flag was a mixture of black and white; when these two primary colors are combined, they produce a single color, gray. There have been many references to the stone for the Gad tribe being jasper or agate.

  However, hematite, which is an iron ore of a silvery gray-black color and symbolizes

> courage, is the more accurate stone. Physical healing properties include leg cramps, blood disorders, nervous disorders, and insomnia. Also used for purposes of encouraging spinal alignment and the proper healing of bones, breaks, and fractures. Metaphysically, it is used to direct balancing, and it grounds energy to the spirit.

Throughout history, restoration always leads to reformation (a change that makes things better), which releases new thought patterns.[4] Little did I know that along with a renewed mindset came a renewed spirit. God has been preparing me for HIM. With each and every experience, HE was breaking me and molding me to serve HIM while revealing and confirming my true identity. Each experience has meaning and a purpose! No one can tell me that God does not deliver when it comes to giving us the desires of our heart. God is TRULY awesome and mystifying! He is patient and persistent at the same time! He creates us

---

[4] Craig A. Ponder Sr., CEA, *Cracking the Apostolic & Prophetic Code* (Texas: Palm Tree Publications, 2008), 86.

ALL with a purpose, and patiently waits for us to come into the full understanding of not only who HE is, but also who we are in HIM. Although He gives us the right to choose our paths in making our own choices to serve Him or not, nothing takes place without His knowledge! He knows us better than we know ourselves, knowing each step that we are going to take before we take it. This applies to our mistakes as well as our accomplishments, and our hesitations and procrastinations.

He orchestrates the events in our lives with the intent of steering us in the right direction for His Glory at the most opportune time for the revealing and unveiling of HIS truth. Our lives are predestined, meaning, as odd as it may sound, that God planned the events of our lives long before we were conceived in our mothers' wombs! HE knew exactly what skills and character traits HE wanted to bless us with so that we could carry out HIS mission for the edification of HIS kingdom! God is calling us to be courageous, and more than just conquerors. He does not wish for any of us to perish, but to have everlasting life!

FROM WHAT TRIBE WERE YOU BIRTHED?

Dear Lord, I pray to you in the name of Jesus Christ to challenge each person reading this book to identify his or her true calling and to embrace it!

> *Blessed is the man that walketh not in the counsel of the ungodly, nor standeth in the way of sinners, nor sitteth in the seat of the scornful. But his delight is in the law of the Lord; and in his law doth he meditate day and night. And he shall be like a tree planted by the rivers of water, that bringeth forth his fruit in his season; his leaf also shall not wither; and whatsoever he doeth shall prosper.*
>
> **- Psalms 1:1-3**

CHAPTER 7

BONUS

*But the Lord hath taken you,
and brought you forth out of the iron furnace,
even out of Egypt, to be unto him a people
of inheritance, as ye are this day.*

- DEUTERONOMY 4:20

FROM WHAT TRIBE WERE YOU BIRTHED?

October 10, 2013

Hematite (also spelled haematite) is **iron oxide,** and the chemical composition is represented as Fe_2O_3. Hematite gets its name from *haima,* the Greek word for blood, and it is considered one of the most important iron-ore minerals. It is a powerful stone for grounding and repelling negativity. When used in healing, it works to assist circulation through its magnetic properties while also encouraging the absorption of iron and the production of healthy red blood cells. It purifies, oxygenates, and revitalizes the bodily fluids, thereby nurturing blood for the entire body.

In this way, this mineral is excellent for the kidneys and anemia, and for tissue regeneration. It is thought to have an overall calming effect on the nervous system and can reduce stress, thus making it helpful for insomnia and anxiety in addition to increasing one's sense of courage and self-esteem. It is a good stone for communication and for those learning how to meditate. It acts as an overall stabilizing force to balance the mind, body, and spirit. When carried or worn as jewelry, it actually absorbs potentially hazardous vibrations in keeping that negative energy from overwhelming your spirit. Your Hematite, whether worn as a piece of jewelry or carried, should be cleansed regularly in salt water. If not, it will eventually break and crack into little pieces after it has served its purpose!

> ***Iron sharpeneth iron; so a man sharpeneth the countenance of his friend.***
>
> **- Proverbs 27:17**

◆ ◆ ◆

God repeatedly tells us through HIS word of truth that HE has given us everything that we would ever need to be successful and victorious until the return of our Savior, Lord and Master, Jesus Christ! For example, after experiencing the power of this mineral to diminish the absorption of harmful negative energy that weakens my immune system, I have purchased approximately five or more bracelets at a time to always have on hand. Prior to becoming aware of the supernatural healing properties of hematite, my spirit was adversely affected by the volatile energy within my working environment. On many occasions, I would get agitated and frustrated for no apparent reason, and some days I would be extremely tired and worn down. There were days of intense headaches and uncontrollable muscle twitching on the left side of my face from my eye and jaw area. Picking up the emotions of others, I would feel sad and would sometimes cry throughout the day, not knowing that I had a gift as an intercessor. Today, my eyes, ears, and heart are open to hearing the voice of God, allowing HIM to reveal the many hidden treasures and aid me in pursuing and carrying out HIS mission and purpose for my life.

Thy shoes shall be iron and brass; and as thy days, so shall thy strength be.

- Deuteronomy 33:25

◆ ◆ ◆

Hematite is a very common and inexpensive stone, but like anything else as it pertains to supply and demand, once others come to know the powerful healing effects of this mineral, it will become hard to get and will be quite expensive. A similar mineral called magnetite is also a common iron oxide mineral with the following chemical composition of Fe_3O_4, which offers more of a magnetic pull. It is named after an ancient region of Greece where metal production was prominent.

THESSALONIANS 2:[13-14] **Meanwhile, we've got our hands full continually thanking God for you, our good friends—so loved by God! God picked you out as his from the very start. Think of it: included in God's original plan of salvation by the bond of faith in the living truth. This is the life of the Spirit he invited you to through the Message we delivered, in which you get in on the glory of our Master, Jesus Christ.** [15-17] **So, friends, take a firm stand, feet on the ground and head high. Keep a tight grip on what you were taught, whether in personal conversation or by our letter. May Jesus himself and God our Father, who reached out in love and surprised you with gifts of unending help and confidence, put a fresh heart in you, invigorate your work, enliven your speech. - (MSG)**

APPENDECIES

BIBLICAL REFERENCES TO THE MONTHS

Exodus (Shemot) 12:1-4 ~ *And the Lord spake unto Moses and Aaron in the land of Egypt saying, this month shall be unto you the beginning of months: it shall be the first month of the year to you. Speak ye unto all the congregation of Israel, saying, In the tenth day of this month they shall take to them every man a lamb, according to the house of their fathers, a lamb for an house: And if the household be too little for the lamb, let him and his neighbour next unto his house take it according to the number of the souls; every man according to his eating shall make your count for the lamb.*

The Children of Israel used the names of their God-given calendar for hundreds of years. After the Jews were exiled from Judah to Babylonia in 586 BC, they adopted Babylonian names for the months of the year. Many of the months' names were changed, such as Abib to Nisan, Zif to Iyar, Ethanim to Tishri, and Bul to Cheshvan.

Month One: *Nisan* or *Abib/Aviv* (30 days)

- ***Nisan*** - The name of the month was changed from *Abib* to **Nisan,** meaning "their flight" after the Babylonian Captivity (***Nehemiah 2:1***). *Abib* signifies the first harvest or first fruit, which was barley (grain). It is also referenced as the *Abib* for the month of newly ripened grain, and the ear of grain, or the ear of corn.

- Exodus 13:4 - This day came ye out in the month Abib.

- Exodus 23:15 - You shall keep the Feast of Unleavened Bread; you shall eat unleavened bread seven days, as I commanded you, in the time appointed in the month Abib; for in it you came out from Egypt; and none shall appear before me empty.

- Exodus 34:18 - The Feast of Unleavened Bread shall you keep. Seven days you shall eat unleavened bread, as I commanded you, in the time of the month Abib; for in the month Abib you came out from Egypt.

- Deuteronomy 16:1 - Observe the month of Abib, and keep the Passover to the Lord your God; for in the month of b the Lord your God brought you out of Egypt by night.

- Numbers 9:1 - And the Lord spake unto Moses in the wilderness of Sinai, in the first month of the second year after they were come out of the land of Egypt, saying,

- Nehemiah 2:1 - And it came to pass in the month Nisan, in the twentieth year of Artakhshist the king, that wine was before him; and I took up the wine, and gave it to the king. Now I had never been sad before in his presence.

- Esther 3:7 - In the first month, that is, the month Nisan, in the twelfth year of king Ahasuerus, they cast Pur, that is, the lot, before Haman from day to day, and from month to month, to the twelfth month, that is, the month Adar.

FROM WHAT TRIBE WERE YOU BIRTHED?

Month Two: *Iyar/Iyyar* or *Zif/Ziv* (29 days)

- Genesis 7:11 - In the six hundredth year of Noah's life, in the second month, the seventeenth day of the month, the same day were all the fountains of the great deep broken up, and the windows of heaven were opened.

- Genesis 8:14 - And in the second month, on the seven and twentieth day of the month, was the Earth dried.

- Exodus 16:1 - And they took their journey from Elim, and all the congregation of the children of Israel came unto the wilderness of Sin, which is between Elim and Sinai, on the fifteenth day of the second month after their departing out of the land of Egypt.

- Numbers 1:1 - And the Lord spake unto Moses in the wilderness of Sinai, in the tabernacle of the congregation, on the first day of the second month, in the second year after they were come out of the land of Egypt ...

- Numbers 1:18 - And they assembled all the congregation together on the first day of the second month, and they declared their pedigrees after their families, by the house of their fathers, according to the number of the names, from twenty years old and upward, by their polls.

- Numbers 9:11 - The fourteenth day of the second month at even they shall keep it, and eat it with unleavened bread and bitter herbs.

- Numbers 10:11 - And it came to pass on the twentieth day of the second month, in the second year, that the cloud was taken up from off the tabernacle of the testimony.

- 1 Kings 6:1 - And it came to pass in the four hundred and eightieth* year after the people of Israel came out of the land of Egypt, in the fourth year of Solomon's reign over Israel, in the month Ziv, which is the second month, that he began to build the house of the Lord.

FROM WHAT TRIBE WERE YOU BIRTHED?

- 1 Kings 6:37 - In the fourth year was the foundation of the house of the Lord laid, in the month Ziv.

- 1 Chronicles 27:4 - And over the course of the second month was Dodai an Ahohite, and of his course was Mikloth also the ruler: in his course likewise were twenty and four thousand.

- 2 Chronicles 3:2 - And he began to build in the second day of the second month, in the fourth year of his reign.

- 2 Chronicles 30:2 - For the king had taken counsel, and his princes, and all the congregation in Jerusalem, to keep the passover in the second month.

- 2 Chronicles 30:13 - And there assembled at Jerusalem much people to keep the feast of unleavened bread in the second month, a very great congregation.

- 2 Chronicles 30:15 - Then they killed the passover on the fourteenth day of the second month: and the priests and the Levites were ashamed, and sanctified themselves, and brought in the burnt offerings into the house of the Lord.

- Ezra 3:8 - Now in the second year of their coming unto the house of God at Jerusalem, in the second month, began Zerubbabel the son of Shealtiel, and Jeshua the son of Jozadak, and the remnant of their brethren the priests and the Levites, and all they that were come out of the captivity unto Jerusalem; and appointed the Levites, from twenty years old and upward, to set forward the work of the house of the Lord.

Month Three: Sivan/Siwan (30 days)

- Exodus 19:1 - In the third month, when the children of Israel were gone forth out of the land of Egypt, the same day came they into the wilderness of Sinai.

- 1 Chronicles 27:5 - The third captain of the host for the third month was Benaiah the son of Jehoiada, a chief priest: and in his course were twenty and four thousand.

FROM WHAT TRIBE WERE YOU BIRTHED?

- 2 Chronicles 15:10 - So they gathered themselves together at Jerusalem in the third month, in the fifteenth year of the reign of Asa.

- 2 Chronicles 31:7 - In the third month they began to lay the foundation of the heaps, and finished them in the seventh month.

- Esther 8:9 - Then were the king's scribes called at that time in the third month, that is, the month Sivan, on the three and twentieth day thereof; and it was written according to all that Mordecai commanded unto the Jews, and to the lieutenants, and the deputies and rulers of the provinces which are from India unto Ethiopia, an hundred twenty and seven provinces, unto every province according to the writing thereof, and unto every people after their language, and to the Jews according to their writing, and according to their language.

- Ezekiel 31:1 - And it came to pass in the eleventh year, in the third month, in the first day of the month, that the word of the Lord came unto me ...

Month Four: *Tammuz* (29 days)

- Ezekiel 1:1 - Now it came to pass in the thirtieth year, in the fourth month, in the fifth day of the month, as I was among the captives by the river of Chebar, that the heavens were opened, and I saw visions of God.

- Jeremiah 52:6 - And in the fourth month, in the ninth day of the month, the famine was sore in the city, so that there was no bread for the people of the land.

Month Five: Av/Ab (30 days)

- No scriptural reference

Month Six: *Elul* (29 days)

- Nehemiah 6:15 - So the wall was finished in the twenty fifth day of the month **Elul**, in fifty two days.

- 1 Chronicles 27:9 - The sixth captain for the sixth month was Ira the son of Ikkesh the

Tekoite: and in his course were twenty and four thousand.

- Ezekiel 8:1 - And it came to pass in the sixth year, in the sixth month, in the fifth day of the month, as I sat in mine house, and the elders of Judah sat before me, that the hand of the Lord GOD fell there upon me.

- Haggai 1:1 - In the second year of Darius the king, in the sixth month, in the first day of the month, came the word of the Lord by Haggai the prophet unto Zerubbabel the son of Shealtiel, governor of Judah, and to Joshua the son of Josedech, the high priest, saying,

- Haggai 1:15 - In the four and twentieth day of the sixth month, in the second year of Darius the king.

- Luke 1:26-28 - And in the sixth month the angel Gabriel was sent from God unto a city of Galilee, named Nazareth, to a virgin espoused to a man whose name was Joseph, of the house of David; and the virgin's name was Mary. And the angel came in unto her, and said, Hail, thou that art highly favoured, the Lord is with thee: blessed art thou among women.

- Luke 1:36 - And, behold, thy cousin Elisabeth, she hath also conceived a son in her old age: and this is the sixth month with her, who was called barren.

Month Seven: *Tishri/Tishrei* or *Ethanim* (30 days)

- 1 Kings 8:2 - And all the men of Israel assembled themselves to King Solomon at the feast in the month of **Ethanim**, which is the seventh month.

Month Eight: *Cheshvan/Heshvan* or *Bul* (29 or 30 days)

- 1 Kings 6:38 - And in the eleventh year, in the month **Bul**, which is the eighth month, was the house finished in all its parts, and according to all its specifications. And he was seven years in building it.

- Zechariah 1:1 - In the eighth month, in the second year of Darius, came the word of the Lord unto Zechariah, the son of Berechiah, the son of Iddo the prophet ...

Month Nine: *Kislev/Chislev/Chisleu* (29 or 30 days)

The name Kislev is derived from the Hebrew word for "security and trust."

- Zechariah 7:1 - And it came to pass in the fourth year of king Darius, that the word of the Lord came to Zechariah on the fourth day of the ninth month, which is Kislev.

- Nehemiah 1:1 - The words of Nehemiah the son of Hachaliah. And it came to pass in the month Kislev, in the twentieth year, when I was in Shushan the capital ...

- Haggai 2:10 - In the four and twentieth day of the ninth month, in the second year of Darius, came the word of the Lord by Haggai the prophet ...

Month Ten: *Tevet*/*Tebeth* (29 days)

- Esther 2:16 - So Esther was taken to king Ahasuerus to his royal palace in the tenth month, which is the month **Tebeth**, in the seventh year of his reign.

Month Eleven: *Shevat*/*Shebat* (30 days)

- Zechariah 1:7 - On the twenty fourth day of the eleventh month, which is the month **Shebat**, in the second year of Darius, the word of the Lord came to Zechariah, the son of Berechiah, the son of Iddo the prophet ...

Month Twelve: *Adar* I (28 days):

The word Adar is cognate (related) to the word "*adir*" meaning "strength." *Adar* literally means "exalted, praised, power and strength," where it says: "the Lord is (*Adir*) mighty on High."

- Esther 3:7 - In the first month, that is, the month Nisan, in the twelfth year of king Ahasuerus, they cast Pur, that is, the lot,

FROM WHAT TRIBE WERE YOU BIRTHED?

before Haman from day to day, and from month to month, to the twelfth month, that is, the month **Adar**.

- Esther 3:13 - And the letters were sent by couriers to all the king's provinces, to destroy, to kill, and to annihilate all Jews, both young and old, little children and women, in one day, on the thirteenth day of the twelfth month, which is the month **Adar**, and to plunder their goods.

- Esther 8:12 - On one day in all the provinces of King Ahasuerus, on the thirteenth day of the twelfth month, which is the month **Adar**.

- Esther 9:1 - And in the twelfth month, that is, the month **Adar**, on the thirteenth day of the same, when the king's command and his decree drew near to be put in execution, in the day that the enemies of the Jews hoped to have power over them, though it was turned to the contrary, that the Jews had rule over those who hated them.

- Esther 9:15-21 - For the Jews who were in Shushan gathered themselves together also on the fourteenth day of the month **Adar**, and slew three hundred men at Shushan; but on the plunder they did not lay their hand. On the thirteenth day of the month **Adar**; and on the fourteenth day of the same they rested, and made it a day of feasting and gladness. Therefore the Jews of the villages, who lived in the unwalled towns, make the fourteenth day of the month **Adar** a day of gladness and feasting, and a holiday, and of sending portions one to another. To establish this among them, that they should keep the fourteenth day of the month **Adar**, and the fifteenth day of the same, yearly.

- Ezra 6:15 - And this house was finished on the third day of the month **Adar**, which was in the sixth year of the reign of Darius, the king.

FROM WHAT TRIBE WERE YOU BIRTHED?

SCRIPTURES: THE GAD TRIBE

DEUTERONOMY 27:

THE CURSES TO BE PRONOUNCED ON MOUNT EBAL

13 And these shall stand upon mount Ebal to curse; Reuben, **Gad**, and Asher, and Zebulun, Dan, and Naphtali. 14 And the Levites shall speak, and say unto all the men of Israel with a loud voice, 15 Cursed [be] the man that maketh [any] graven or molten image, an abomination unto the LORD, the work of the hands of the craftsman, and putteth [it] in [a] secret [place]. And all the people shall answer and say, Amen. 16 Cursed [be] he that setteth light by his father or his mother. And all the people shall say, Amen. 17 Cursed [be] he that removeth his neighbour's landmark. And all the people shall say, Amen. 18 Cursed [be] he that maketh the blind to wander out of the way. And all the people shall say, Amen. 19 Cursed [be] he that perverteth the judgment of the stranger, fatherless, and widow. And all the people shall say, Amen.

20 Cursed [be] he that lieth with his father's wife; because he uncovereth his father's skirt. And all the people shall say, Amen. **21** Cursed [be] he that lieth with any manner of beast. And all the people shall say, Amen. **22** Cursed [be] he that lieth with his sister, the daughter of his father, or the daughter of his mother. And all the people shall say, Amen. **23** Cursed [be] he that lieth with his mother in law. And all the people shall say, Amen. **24** Cursed [be] he that smiteth his neighbour secretly. And all the people shall say, Amen. **25** Cursed [be] he that taketh reward to slay an innocent person. And all the people shall say, Amen. **26** Cursed [be] he that confirmeth not [all] the words of this law to do them. And all the people shall say, Amen.

DEUTERONOMY 33:

20 And of Gad he said, Blessed [be] he that enlargeth **Gad**: he dwelleth as a lion, and teareth the arm with the crown of the head. **21** And he provided the first part for himself, because there, [in] a portion of the lawgiver, [was he] seated; and he came with the heads of the people, he executed the justice of the LORD, and his judgments with Israel.

JOSHUA 13: The bounds of the inheritance of Gad

24 And Moses gave [inheritance] unto the tribe of Gad, [even] unto the children of Gad according to their families. **25** And their coast was Jazer, and all the cities of Gilead, and half the land of the children of Ammon, unto Aroer that [is] before Rabbah; **26** And from Heshbon unto Ramathmizpeh, and Betonim; and from Mahanaim unto the border of Debir; **27** And in the valley, Betharam, and Bethnimrah, and Succoth, and Zaphon, the rest of the kingdom of Sihon king of Heshbon, Jordan and [his] border, [even] unto the edge of the sea of Chinnereth on the other side Jordan eastward. [NET Notes, TSK]

28 This [is] the inheritance of the children of Gad after their families, the cities, and their villages.

EZEKIEL 48: 27:

And by the border of Zebulun, from the east side unto the west side, Gad a [portion]. **28** And by the border of Gad, at the south side southward, the border shall be even from Tamar [unto] the waters of strife [in] Kadesh, [and] to the river toward the great sea.

RELEVATION 7: 5:

Of the tribe of Juda [were] sealed twelve thousand. Of the tribe of Reuben [were] sealed twelve thousand. Of the tribe of Gad [were] sealed twelve thousand.

CRYSTAL/GEMSTONE HEALING

What many people fail to realize is the constructional composition of gemstones, which are also referred to as crystals. Gemstones are the formation of minerals that come together to form a solid, rock-like structure that also has healing properties. The study of the use of minerals in medicine is known as lithotherapy, and although there is no scientific proof behind any of the suggested remedies, there are still hundreds of thousands of people who believe in the mystical powers of crystal healing. For severe back pains, it is recommended that one should carry a piece of snowflake obsidian and hematite in his pocket.

Arthritis: Gems associated with helping alleviate the pain of arthritis, although totally unproven, include: apatite, aquamarine, amber, garnet, pyrite, and tourmaline.

Eyes: Gems associated with helping prevent and cure problems with sight, although totally unproven, include: aquamarine, emerald, eye agate, chalcedony, onyx, and sapphire.

Headaches: Gems associated with helping prevent and cure headaches, although totally unproven, include: amethyst, azurite, diamond, lapis lazuli, malachite, moonstone, emerald, and tiger's eye.

Heart Ailments: Gems associated with helping blood circulation, although totally unproven, include: aventurine, carnelian, morganite, rhodonite garnet, rose quartz, ruby, topaz, and turquoise.

Pancreas: Gems associated with aiding the pancreas, although totally unproven, include: amethyst, citrine, garnet, moonstone, obsidian, and green tourmaline.

Sciatica: Gems associated with helping your sciatica, although totally unproven, include: amethyst, citrine, diamond, emerald, jasper, carnelian, pearl, rose quartz, peridot, ruby, and tiger's eye.

Sore Throats: Gems associated with helping prevent and cure sore throats, although totally unproven, include: opals, sodalite, and blue topaz. Silver is also said to help alleviate sore throats.

Stomach: Gems associated with aiding stomach problems, although totally unproven, include: tiger's eye, pyrite, red jasper, malachite, rhodochrosite.

FROM WHAT TRIBE WERE YOU BIRTHED?

In addition, many crystal healers claim that the following gems are useful: agates for upset stomachs, amazonite to increase stamina, ametrine to relieve depression, carnelian to improve appetite, emeralds to relieve back pains, imperial topaz to increase metabolism, and fluorite to alleviate joint problems.

ANN GWEN MACK

GEMSTONE REMEDIES FROM A-Z

ABUNDANCE Chrysoprase, Citrine, Golden Calcite, Emerald

ABUSE- Pink Tourmaline, Rose Quartz, Thulite, Larimar

ACNE- Cuprite, Larimar, Rose Quartz

ADDICTION- Avalonite, Crysocolla with Cuprite, Malachite-Azurite, Peridot

ADRENAL GLANDS- Kansas Pop Rocks, Sulfur, Kyanite, Black Tourmaline

AGING—Emerald, Rose Quartz, Rutilated Quartz, Boulder Opal

ALCOHOLISM- Avalonite, Crysocolla with Cuprite, Golden Calcite, Peridot, Phenacite

ALLERGIC REACTIONS- Bloodstone, Hematite

ALTITUDE SICKNESS- Hematite, Jet

ALZHEIMER'S- Blue Chalcedony, Fluorite

ANEMIA- Hematite, Garnet, Bloodstone

ANGELIC CONTACT- Angelite, Celestite, Kunzite, Scolecite

FROM WHAT TRIBE WERE YOU BIRTHED?

ANGER- Black Tourmaline, Chrysocolla, Peridot, Oligoclase

ANOREXIA- Rose Quartz, Thulite, Golden Calcite, Malachite

ANXIETY- Aventurine, Lepidolite, Amethyst, Amazonite

ARTHRITIS- Boji Stones, Chrysocolla, Lapis Lazuli, Imperial Topaz

ASSERTIVENESS- Chrysoprase, Golden Calcite, Tigers Eye

ASTHMA- Malachite, Vanadinite

ASTRAL PROJECTION- Angelite, Hawks Eye, Hour Glass Selenite, Time-Link Crystal

ATTENTION DEFICIT DISORDER- Fluorite, Hour Glass Selenite, Selenite, Azurite

BACKACHE- Amber, Green Tourmaline, DT Quartz

BACTERIAL INFECTION- Anhydrite, Malachite, Sulfur

BIPOLAR DISEASE- Kunzite, Rutilated Quartz

ANN GWEN MACK

BIRTHING- Peridot, Shiva Lingham,

BLADDER AND KIDNEYS- Cuprite, Prehnite

BLEEDING-DECREASE- Bloodstone, Malachite, Sodalite, Sapphire

BLISTERS- Anhydrite, Sulfur, Rose Quartz

BLOOD PURIFYING DISORDERS/CIRCULATION- Chiastolite, Garnet, Malachite, Ruby

BLOOD PRESSURE BALANCE- Chiastolite, Malachite, Ruby

BONE MARROW- Malachite, Lapis Lazuli

BOWELS- Lepidolite

BREAST MILK- Carnelian, Chalcedony, Chiastolite, Turquoise

BREATHLESSNESS- Amber, Vanadinite

BROKEN BONES- Axinite, Calcite, Green Tourmaline, Topaz, Selenite

BRONCHITIS- Aquamarine, Chrysocolla, Amazonite, Aventurine

BURN OUT- Garnet, Ruby, Vanadinite, Zincite

FROM WHAT TRIBE WERE YOU BIRTHED?

BURNS- Boji Stones, Chrysocolla, Blue-Lace Agate

BURSITIS- Amber, Blue-Lace Agate

CALMING- Manganocalcite, Angelite,

CANCER- Lepidolite, Sugilite, Red Jasper, Watermelon Tourmaline

CATARACTS- Green Apophyllite

CHEMOTHERAPY- Malachite, Sulfur, Anhydrite

CHICKENPOX- Childrenite

CHILD ABUSE RECOVERY- Manganocalcite, Kunzite, Green Fluorite

CHILDBIRTH- Shiva Lingham, Hematite, Ruby, Bloodstone, Opal

CHRONIC FATIGUE SYNDROME- Ruby

CIRCULATION- Bustamite, Fire Quartz, Tektite

COMPUTER STRESS- Smoky Quartz

COLIC- Boji Stones, Amber

COLDS/SINUS- Azurite, Amethyst, Fluorite, Kyanite

COMMUNICATION- Amazonite, Blue Calcite,

Turquoise, Oregon Opal

CONCEPTION- Quartz Scepter, Rhodochrosite, Shiva Lingham Stone

CONFIDENCE- Golden Calcite, Orange Calcite, Malachite

CONFUSION- Charoite, Fluorite, Howlite

CONSTIPATION- Ruby, Smoky Quartz, Black Tourmaline

COUGH- Aquamarine, Turquoise, Chrysocolla

COURAGE- Charoite, Chrysoprase, Golden Calcite, Tigers Eye, Sunstone

CRAMPS- Lepidolite , Hematite

CREATIVE BLOCKS- Orange Calcite, Chiastolite, Golden Calcite

DEGENERATIVE NERVE DISEASES- Malachite, Azurite, Rhodochrosite, Lapis, Sapphire, Sodalite

DEPRESSION- Amethyst, Angelite, Elestial Quartz, Holley Blue, Lepidolite, Smoky Quartz, Sugilite

DETOXIFICATION- Malachite, Anhydrite, Sulfur

FROM WHAT TRIBE WERE YOU BIRTHED?

DIABETES- **Citrine**, Anhydrite, Jade

DIARRHEA- Black Tourmaline, Smoky Quartz

DIGESTION- Amber, Citrine, Sulfur

DIVINATION- Crystal Ball, Obsidian

DREAMWORK- Bustamite, Herkimer diamond, Holley Blue,

DRUG ISSUES- Smoky Quartz, Jet, Tigers Eye, Rutilated Quartz

DYSLEXIA- Sugilite

EARACHE- Amber, Amazonite

EATING DISORDERS- Rose Quartz, Avalonite, Thulite

ECZEMA- Blue Sapphire

EMOTIONAL HEALING- Isis Crystal, Malachite

ENDOCRINE GLANDS- Pietersite, Topaz,

ENVIRONMENTAL POLLUTION- Anhydrite, Sulfur, Zincite

EPILEPSY- Red Jasper, Carnelian, Malachite, Coral, Golden Beryl, Emerald

EYE PROBLEMS- Obsidian, Topaz, Tigers Eye,

Jade, Opal, Obsidian

FATIGUE- Barite, Red Calcite, Vanadinite, Zincite, Peru Opal

FEAR- Angelite, Kunzite, Sunstone, Golden Calcite, Holley Blue, Jet, Lepidolite, Tigers Eye

FEET BURNING- Larimar

FERTILITY (improving) Garnet, Shiva Lingham Stone, Quartz Scepter, Realgar

FEVERS- Brazilianite, Opal, Pietersite, Ruby, Tektite

FIBROMYALGIA- Amethyst, Aventurine, Blue Lace Agate, Citrine, Quartz Crystal, Rose Quartz

FOCUS- Yttrian Fluorite, Fluorite slices,

FORGIVENESS- Angelite

GALLBLADDER- Carnelian, Citrine, Malachite, Emerald, Green Tourmaline

GOUT- Prehnite

GOITER- Amber

GRIEF- Apache Tears, Sugilite, Smoky Quartz, Jet, Elestial Quartz, Angelite, Kyanite

FROM WHAT TRIBE WERE YOU BIRTHED?

GROUNDING- Hematite, Jasper, Mochi Marbles, Obsidian, Smoky Quartz

GUILT- Larimar

GUMS- Agate (all varieties)

HAY FEVER- Blue Lace Agate

HEADACHES- Holley Blue, Aquamarine, Chrysocolla, Turquoise, Sodalite and Blue Tourmaline

HEARING LOSS- Lapis Lazuli

HEART ATTACK- Garnet

HEARTBURN- Dioptase, Peridot, Sulfur

HEART DISEASE- Garnet, Dioptase

HEART HEALING (emotional) Chrysoprase, Danburite, Kunzite, Thulite,

HEAT STROKE- Sunstone

HERPES- Jadeite, Lapis Lazuli

HIP PAIN- Jadeite

HORMONE PRODUCTION- Pietersite, Amethyst

HOT FLASHES- Moonstone, Chrysocolla, Gem

Silica

HYPERTENSION- Chrysocolla

HYPOTHYROIDISM- Blue Tourmaline, Aquamarine, and Anhydrite.

HYSTERIA- Hematite, Obsidian, Smoky Quartz

IMMUNE SYSTEM- Angel Hair Quartz, Herkimer diamond, Rutilated Quartz,

IMPOTENCE- Varascite, Shiva Lingham

INCEST RECOVERY- Avalonite, Thulite, Rose Quartz

INFECTIONS- Sulfur, Anhydrite, Malachite

INFERTILITY- Shiva Lingham Stone, Quartz scepters

INFLAMMATIONS- Pyrite, Chrysocolla

INSOMNIA- Amethyst, Labradorite, Smoky Quartz, Celestite

INTELLECT- Imperial Topaz, Hiddenite

INTESTINES- Thulite, Brown Tourmaline

INTUITION- Amethyst, Azurite, Selenite

IRRITABILITY- Amethyst, Blue Lace Agate,

FROM WHAT TRIBE WERE YOU BIRTHED?

Turquoise

ITCHING- Chrysocolla

JEALOUSY- Peridot

JET LAG- Hematite, Black Tourmaline

JOINT SORENESS- Green Calcite, Hiddenite

JOY- Blue Sapphire, Sunstone, Vanadinite

LACTATION- Carnelian, Chalcedony, Chiastolite, Turquoise

LARYNGITIS- Stilbite

LEARNING DIFFICULTIES- Fluorite, Azurite

LEG CRAMPS- Jadeite, Lepidolite

LEUKEMIA- Chrysocolla

LIVER- Danburite, Imperial Topaz, Opal

LONELINESS- Shiva Lingham, Thulite

LOVE- Thulite, Rose Quartz, Manganocalcite, Stellar Ice Calcite,

LUNGS- Bustamite, Garnet, Pyrite

MEASLES- Turquoise

MEDITATION- Amethyst, Fluorite, Holley Blue, Lapis Lazuli, Moonstone, Record Keeper Quartz,

MEMORY PROBLEMS- Yttrian Fluorite

MENIERE'S DISEASE- Dioptase, Diopside

MENOPAUSE- Moonstone, Carnelian

MENSTRUAL CRAMPS- Carnelian, Cuprite, Moonstone,

MENTAL CONFUSION/DISORDERS- Apophyllite, Fluorite, Danburite

MIGRAINES- Aquamarine, Chrysocolla, Turquoise, Sodalite and Blue Tourmaline

MISCARRIAGE (prevention)- Shiva Lingham Stones, Carnelian, Ruby, Aquamarine

MISCARRIAGE (recovery)- Chrysocolla

MORNING SICKNESS- Moonstone, Red Jasper, Malachite, Sodalite, Oligoclase

MUMPS- Aquamarine, Topaz

MUSCLE ACHES- Diopside, Jadeite, Lepidolite

MULTIPLE SCLEROSIS- Lapis, Sodalite, Blue Sapphire, Moonstone, Amethyst

NAIL PROBLEMS- Apatite

NAUSEA- Green Calcite, Peridot, Golden Calcite

FROM WHAT TRIBE WERE YOU BIRTHED?

NERVOUSNESS- Barite, Sodalite, Watermelon Tourmaline

NEURALGIA- Lapis, Carnelian, Amber

NOSE BLEED- Carnelian

NURTURING- Shiva Lingham, Thulite, Manganocalcite

OBESITY- Avalonite, Heulandite

OSTEOPOROSIS- Amazonite, Calcite, Selenite

PAIN- Peridot, Jet, Smoky Quartz, Amber

PANCREAS- Herderite

PARKINSON'S DISEASE- Opal

PAST LIFE REGRESSION- Kunzite, Apophyllite

PEACE- Angelite, Blue Calcite, Celestite, Kyanite

PNEUMONIA- Fluorite

POISON IVY- Serpentine

POLARITY BALANCING- Kunzite, Rutilated Quartz

PREMENSTRUAL SYNDROME- Moonstone, Jade, Chrysocolla, Turquoise, Kunzite

PROBLEM SOLVING- Moonstone, Scolecite,

PROSPERITY- Angelite, Blue Sapphire, Citrine, Varascite

PROTECTION- Amber, Black Tourmaline, Chiastolite, Hematite, Hawks Eye, Mochi Marbles, Obsidian

PROSTATE GLAND- Zincite

PSORIASIS- Sulfur, Green Tourmaline, Rhodochrosite

PSYCHIATRIC DISORDERS- Diopside

PSYCHIC DEVELOPMENT- Azurite, Fluorite, Iolite

RAPE RECOVERY- Lapis, Chrysocolla, Black Tourmaline

RASH- Larimar, Blue Calcite, Blue Lace Agate, Angelite

REPRODUCTIVE ORGANS- Orange Tourmaline, Rubellite Tourmaline,

RELATIONSHIPS- Brazilianite, Peridot, Manganocalcite, Kyanite,

RELAXATION- Blue Lace Agate, Turquoise

FROM WHAT TRIBE WERE YOU BIRTHED?

RESPIRATORY SYSTEM- Coral, Topaz, Amber, Tigers Eye, Zircon, Agate

RHEUMATISM- Boji Stones, Imperial Topaz

SCIATICA- Green Tourmaline, Kyanite, Smoky Quartz

SCRYING- Crystal Ball, Obsidian

SELF-ESTEEM/WORTH- Golden Calcite, Isis crystal, Oregon Opal

SELF-SABOTAGE- Golden Calcite, Rose Quartz, Thulite, Avalonite

SHINGLES- Green Tourmaline, Black Tourmaline, Kyanite

SHOCK- Bloodstone, Larimar, Sunstone

SHYNESS- Golden Calcite, Orange Calcite, Hessonite Garnet

SIGHT- Obsidian, Topaz, Tigers Eye, Jade, Opal, Obsidian

SINUS PROBLEMS- Azurite, Blue Lace Agate

SKIN, NAILS, AND HAIR- Bustamite, Lepidolite

SMELL- Hessonite Garnet

SMOKING CESSATION- Smoky Quartz, Staurolite

SORE THROAT- Blue Lace Agate, Blue Calcite, Angelite

SPRAINS- Sphene, Green Calcite, Aventurine, DT Quartz

SPINE- Tigers Eye, Labradorite, Selenite, Calcite, Magnetite

SPIRITUAL DEVELOPMENT- Amethyst, Apophyllite, Azurite, Celestite, Epidote, Fluorite, Holley Blue, Iolite, Hour Glass Selenite, Selenite,

STAGE FRIGHT- Golden Calcite, Aquamarine, Amethyst

STDS- Tektite, Chrysoprase

STOMACH- Holley Blue, Sunstone, Jet, Peridot, Varascite

STRESS- Amethyst, Angelite, Aventurine

SURGICAL RECOVERY- Amber, Smoky Quartz, Jasper, Chrysocolla, Chrysoprase

SWELLING- Peridot, Emerald, Green

FROM WHAT TRIBE WERE YOU BIRTHED?

Tourmaline, Aquamarine, Sapphire, Sodalite

TEETH- Calcite, Selenite, Sphene

TELEPATHY- Celestite, Azurite, Selenite, Apophyllite

THROAT- Blue Lace Agate, Citrine, Turquoise

THYROID BALANCE- Citrine, Halite

TRAUMA- Aventurine, Citrine, Blue Lace Agate, Malachite

TRUST- Axinite, Hiddenite, Lepidolite, Oligoclase

TUBERCULOSIS- Morganite

TUMORS- Malachite, Bloodstone, Smoky Quartz

ULCER- Sunstone, Peridot, Lepidolite, Smithsonite

URINARY TRACT INFECTION- Blue Sapphire, Kyanite

VARICOSE VEINS- Amber, Blue Lace Agate, Bloodstone

VERTIGO- Cuprite, Lapis Lazuli, Elestial Quartz,

VISION WORK (visualization)- Rutilated

Quartz,

VITALITY- Garnet, Vanadinite, Sunstone

VOMITING- Lapis Lazuli

WARMING- Imperial Topaz, Vanadinite, Ruby, Garnet, Zincite

WATER RETENTION- Chrysocolla, Cuprite

WHOOPING COUGH- Amber, Blue Lace Agate, Topaz

WISDOM- Apophyllite, Avalonite, Holley Blue Agate, Oregon Opal, Sodalite

FROM WHAT TRIBE WERE YOU BIRTHED?

LISTING OF CHEMICAL ELEMENTS

Only about four percent of the total mass of the universe is made of atoms or ions, and thus represented by chemical elements.

A chemical element is a pure chemical substance that consists of a single type of atom distinguished by its atomic number, which is the number of protons in its atomic nucleus. Elements are divided into metals, metalloids and nonmetals.

SYMBOL	CHEMICAL ELEMENT	ATOMIC WEIGHT
Ac	Actinium	227
Al	Aluminum	27
Am	Americium	243
Sb	Antimony	122
Ar	Argon	40
As	Arsenic	75
At	Astatine	210
Ba	Barium	137
Bk	Berkelium	247
Be	Beryllium	9
Bi	Bismuth	209
Bh	Bohrium	264
B	Boron	11
Br	Bromine	80
Cd	Cadmium	112

SYMBOL	CHEMICAL ELEMENT	ATOMIC WEIGHT
Cs	Caesium	133
Ca	Calcium	40
Cf	Californium	251
C	Carbon	12
Ce	Cerium	140
Cl	Chlorine	35.5
Cr	Chromium	52
Co	Cobalt	59
Cu	Copper	64
Cm	Curium	247
Ds	Darmstadtium	271
Db	Dubnium	262
Dy	Dysprosium	162.5
Es	Einsteinium	254
Er	Erbium	167
Eu	Europium	152
Fm	Fermium	253
F	Fluorine	19
Fr	Francium	223
Gd	Gadolinium	157
Ga	Gallium	70
Ge	Germanium	73
Au	Gold	197
Hf	Hafnium	178.5
Hs	Hassium	277
He	Helium	4
Ho	Holmium	165
H	Hydrogen	1

FROM WHAT TRIBE WERE YOU BIRTHED?

SYMBOL	CHEMICAL ELEMENT	ATOMIC WEIGHT
In	Indium	115
I	Iodine	127
Ir	Iridium	192
Fe	Iron	56
Kr	Krypton	84
La	Lanthanum	139
Lw	Lawrencium	257
Pb	Lead	207
Li	Lithium	7
Lu	Lutetium	175
Mg	Magnesium	24
Mn	Manganese	55
Mt	Meitnerium	268
Md	Mendelevium	256
Hg	Mercury	201
Mo	Molybdenum	96
Nd	Neodymium	144
Ne	Neon	20
Np	Neptunium	237
Ni	Nickel	59
Nb	Niobium	93
N	Nitrogen	14
No	Nobelium	254
Os	Osmium	190
O	Oxygen	16
Pd	Palladium	106
P	Phosphorus	31
Pt	Platinum	195

SYMBOL	CHEMICAL ELEMENT	ATOMIC WEIGHT
Pu	Plutonium	242
Po	Polonium	210
K	Potassium	39
Pr	Praseodymium	141
Pm	Promethium	147
Pa	Protactinium	231
Ra	Radium	226
Rn	Radon	222
Re	Rhenium	186
Rh	Rhodium	103
Rg	Roentgenium	272
Rb	Rubidium	85.5
Ru	Ruthenium	101
Rf	Rutherfordium	261
Sm	Samarium	150
Sc	Scandium	45
Sg	Seaborgium	266
Se	Selenium	79
Si	Silicon	28
Ag	Silver	108
Na	Sodium	23
Sr	Strontium	88
S	Sulphur	32
Ta	Tantalum	181
Tc	Technetium	98
Te	Tellurium	128
Tb	Terbium	159
Tl	Thallium	204

FROM WHAT TRIBE WERE YOU BIRTHED?

SYMBOL	CHEMICAL ELEMENT	ATOMIC WEIGHT
Th	Thorium	232
Tm	Thulium	169
Sn	Tin	119
Ti	Titanium	48
W	Tungsten	184
U	Uranium	238
V	Vanadium	51
Xe	Xenon	131
Yb	Ytterbium	173
Y	Yttrium	89
Zn	Zinc	65
Zr	Zirconium	91

REFERENCES

The New Prophetic Generation:
A Biblical Approach to Mentorship and Spiritual Maturity

Author: Apostle Sherman D. Farmer
ISBN-13: 978-0-692-29749-0

Cracking the Apostolic & Prophetic Code

Author: Craig A. Ponder Sr., CEA
ISBN: 978-0-9817054-3-X

The Bible Educator, Volumes 2

Author: Plumptre, E H (Edward Hayes)
ISBN-13: 978-1152873667

The Crystal Bible:
A Definitive Guide to Crystals

Author: Judy Hall
ISBN: 1582972400

FROM WHAT TRIBE WERE YOU BIRTHED?

The Curious Lore of Precious Stones

Author: Kunz, George Frederic
ISBN-13: 978-1162581194

A Dictionary of Science, Literature and Art

Author: Brande, William Thomas

Love is in the Earth:
A Kaleidoscope of Crystals (Love is in the Earth)

Author: Melody
ISBN: 0962819034

Mazzaroth, Parts 1-4

Author: Frances Rolleston
ISBN-13: 978-0877289463

www.archive.org/details/bibleeducator12plum

www.archive.org/details/curiousloreofpreo28009mbp

www.archive.org/details/dictionaryofscieoobran

www.philologos.org/__eb-mazzaroth/

www.esotericonline.net/group/astrosymbolism/forum/topics/donkeys-in-the-sky-the-constellation-of-cancer-or-the-crab

www.greatsite.com/timeline-english-bible-history/

www.facebook.com/HebrewWordOfTheDay

www.divineviewpoint.com/sane/dbm/ISBE/isbe/isbe_T2.htm

www.kabbalahoflife.com/index.php/month-of-shevat

www.internationalstandardbible.com/S/stones-precious.html

www.britannica.com/EBchecked/topic/582039/Tammuz

www.2-acres.com/Ginger/12_Tribes_of_Israel.pdf

www.mineralminers.com/html/citminfo.htm

ABOUT THE AUTHOR

After finding herself unemployed for the third time, **Ann Gwen Mack** made a conscious commitment to push beyond the boundaries and pursue a degree in Business Management. In spite of her spiritual journey's imaginary glass ceiling, she accomplished this goal in 2002. Though she spent most of her life church and club hopping, she believed there was much more to life than the ups and downs the world had presented.

A native Washingtonian, Ann encountered her first poltergeist experience while volunteering during the World Trade Center disaster. However, it wouldn't be until 2006 that she developed a real relationship with God.

Ann later accepted a position at the U.S. Department of Energy Headquarters in as a participant within the Career Intern Program (CIP) in 2008. On the building's ground floor, she received the gift of speaking in tongues. "Who said there was no place for God in government, on the job, or in a business setting? Most certainly not God!"

Since that time, God told her not to worry about being rewarded or promoted by man for her accomplishments, because she was being commissioned to write for HIM (Psalm 75:6-7), and HE was going to reward her far greater than any monetary value man could ever extend.

Ann has since yielded to her life's calling of ministering the Gospel, published her first book, *What Do I Do with My Pain?: Proclaim Liberty to the Captives* in 2010 and accepted her assignment for introducing others to their connection to the Twelve Tribes of Israel.

To learn more, visit www.AnnGwenMack.com

WE WANT TO HEAR FROM YOU!!!

If this book has made a difference in your life Ann would be delighted to hear about it.

Leave a review on Amazon.com!

BOOK ANN TO SPEAK AT YOUR NEXT EVENT!

Send an email to booking@publishyourgift.com

Learn more about Ann at:
www.AnnGwenMack.com

"EMPOWERING YOU TO IMPACT GENERATIONS"
WWW.PUBLISHYOURGIFT.COM

www.ingramcontent.com/pod-product-compliance
Lightning Source LLC
Chambersburg PA
CBHW071619080526
44588CB00010B/1193